MISSING

A Story of American Merchant Mariners in World War II

Norma Andreasen

This book is dedicated to my father,
Hans Didrik Andreasen,
and to the 59 other souls who lost their lives on the
Esso Williamsburg in September of 1942,
and to my mother,
Anna Cecilia Olesen Andreasen,
who valiantly took over the family helm when our captain was lost.

THE CREW:
Anderson, Morris A.
Andreasen, Hans D.
Baccaro, Michael
Boucher, Fred S.
Brown, Lester T.
Callahan, Dennis F.
Cannes, Felix
Chambers, Fred L.
Cloyd, Cecil T.
Conception, Innocencio C.
Craddock, Isaac L.
DiStefano, Arturo
Driscoll, Florence N.
Fitzgerald, Raymond
Gayle, Lea M.
Geisendaffer, George
Hastings, John W.
Hempenstall, Patrick J.
Herron, Donald B.
Jackson, Reuben
Johnson, Edward F.
Jones, Fred M.

Lally, Albert J.
Lehde, Henry F.
Linton, Harold C.
Madden, Robert E.
Maher, James F.
Mountain, Varise P.
Nash, Roger W.
Navarro, Manuel
Nostdahl, Olaf A.
Palonis, Charles
Partridge, Fenton
Raynard, Stanley W.
Reilly, Richard P.
Richards, Hobart H.
Strawn, Claude A.
Teague, William S.
Tucker, Guthrie K.
Tweed, John
Vennell, Clarence E.
Wentworth, John J.

U. S. NAVY ARMED GUARD
Baker, Glenn H.
Bryant, Donald A.
Byrd, Walter
Gaddy, Reuben R.
Glover, Robert L.
Glover, Stephen F.
Goodrich, Moses H.
Greenwell, John H.
Griffith, Doyle W.
Hamburg, Leo T.
Hicks, Bruce O.
Kindl, Fred J.
Maliszewski, Alexander
Matthews, Glen D.
Mayhew, Merle N.
Mcclintock, Thomas B.
Mealman, Roy E.
Reaves, Iris. V.

CONTENTS

ACKNOWLEDGEMENTS

Acutely aware that there are still so many families and friends of American Merchant Mariners lost in World War II who, as of this date, still have no knowledge of when and how their loved ones died, I've written this book as a key to ways in which the truth can be discovered, even after more than a half century has passed. Books published over the years contain vital, well-documented information on American merchant vessels lost in the war. Archives in the United States, Canada, the United Kingdom and Germany are filled with documents that, when pieced together, tell stories that are heretofore unknown to those most interested. The World Wide Web and related web sites provide an infinite and ongoing source of information and opportunity to contact people whose individual stories, when woven together, reveal what really happened to so many brave souls and their ships.

This book was also made possible by the generous contributions of time, letters, emails, photos, and documents by people desirous of seeing the story of the *Esso Williamsburg* made public for recognition of the sacrifice made by the men of her crew, and for the sake of historical accuracy relating to the sacrifices made by the men of the U. S. Merchant Marines in World War II. Without their help, this story could not have been told:

Bobbie Mosher and her sister Patricia Webb (daughters of Varise Mountain)

Frank Maher (son of James F. Maher, Jr.)

Arthur Mohr of College Station, TX (uncle of Henry (Buddie) Lehde)

Captain Arthur Moore (author of <u>A Careless Word . . . A Needless Sinking</u>)

Katrina Wenger (daughter of Cecil Cloyd, Jr.)

Armond Jones (nephew of Fred McLee Jones)

Matty Loughran (historian of the American Association of American Merchant Marine Veterans, North Atlantic Chapter)

Don Pottie together with Leo Bouchie (nephew of Fred S. Boucher)

Carole Condon (sister of William S. Teague)

Lt. Colonel Kenneth J. Vennell, Illinois Air National Guard (nephew of Clarence Vennell)

Harry Hutson, author and historian, of Cleethorpes, U. K.

Warwick Lister, Florence, Italy (nephew of Harold Cedric Linton)

LeRoy McClelland (John Henry Greenwell, U. S. Naval Armed Guard)

Dick McClintock (Thomas B. McClintock, U. S. Naval Armed Guard)

PROLOGUE

By the end of World War II, 32 American merchant vessels had, quite simply, vanished. The men who sailed them were never heard from again. In 1946, the Standard Oil Company (New Jersey) published *Ships of the Esso Fleet in World War II*, a compendium of war records of 135 tankers owned by the company and its subsidiary, the Panama Transport Company. One article, "All Hands Lost," gives an account of the disappearance of the *Esso Williamsburg* on a voyage to Iceland:

> *In September, 1942, on her way from Aruba to Iceland, with a cargo of Navy fuel, the Esso Williamsburg was lost in the North Atlantic. The circumstances of her sinking are not known.*

The article goes on to relate that:

> *At the outset of her 29th voyage, from which she did not return, the Esso Williamsburg sailed from Aruba on September 12, 1942. She was commanded by Captain Tweed and her engine room was in charge of Chief Engineer Maher. Her cargo of 110,043 barrels of Navy fuel oil was destined for Reykjavik, Iceland, where she was due to arrive about September 24.*

> *On October 24, 1942, the War Shipping Administration reported the vessel and her crew "long overdue and presumed lost as a result of enemy action."*

This book is about the *Esso Williamsburg*, one of 32 merchant ships that disappeared in the fog of World War II, and the fate of the 60 crew members who were on board for its final voyage.

These 60 men represent the 4,720 U. S. Merchant Mariners who are listed as "missing" in World War II. Perishing with the mariners were 1,810 killed or missing members of the U. S. Navy Armed Guard stationed aboard merchant ships that sailed enemy waters carrying food, materiel and troops.

The Newly Commissioned Esso Williamsburg, 1941.

CHAPTER ONE

THE SHIP

May of 1942: then Vice Admiral Karl Dönitz writes in his monthly report to Kriegsmarine headquarters:

> . . . *the U-boats with their extensive war experience are superior to the <U.S.> defense. The American airman see nothing, and the destroyers and patrol vessels proceed at too great a speed to intercept U-boats and likewise having caught one they do not follow up with a tough enough depth charge attack.*

    During these "happy days" of U-boat operations, ships on coastal runs of the United States are constantly in danger. The *Esso Williamsburg* is such a ship. Since the war's inception in December of 1941, she has been racing up and down the Eastern coast of the United States, carrying thousands and thousands of gallons of much-needed oil. Dönitz goes on to state:

> *For each tanker which is shot up the Americans lose not only the oil transport but it affects their new construction adversely. Therefore the sinking of this American transport tonnage seems to me especially important. Also the Americans will be directed to ship their oil by sea at least during the next year. The construction of a supplementary oil pipeline over land connections would take a long time and could not achieve the same results as those attained by the sea route transport.*

Thus, oil tankers are prime targets. As early as February of 1942, U-boats operating along the eastern coast of the U. S. spot the *Esso Williamsburg*. Dönitz's report of February 1 shows the following entry:

Reports on the Enemy: February 1, 1942:

Submarines reported in squares: BE 6654–AM 53– CF 4626–BE 1945 –AE 55–CA 6897–BB 76–CB 1466–CA 5745-8163-5199– DB 3854.

Enemy submarine reports showed: tanker "Esso-Williamburg" (11,400 BRT) in square CA 7332;

How did Dönitz know this?
The U. S. Navy Eastern Sea Frontier Diary for February 1, 1942 shows the following entry:

2240: The SS ESSO WILLIAMSBURG, 37-30N; 75-20W, heading south, sent an SSS.

<Reporting a submarine.>

Duty officer in Norfolk advised

Eagle boat in the vicinity.

The German Kriegsmarine obviously is intercepting messages sent by merchant ships to the U. S. Navy regarding sightings of U-boats. Thus, the ship is in mortal danger while doing her coastal runs.
Preparations for doing even more dangerous work begin in May of 1942, when *Esso Williamsburg* has a permanent degaussing system installed. Enemy forces have been setting up magnetic mine fields in many places along the seaboard. These mines are detonated by magnetic forces from steel ships. A steel ship passing over a mine creates magnetic forces that detonate the mine. Thus, a solution has to be found to counteract the minefields and protect ships from being blown up by them. Degaussing is the answer. Ships are surrounded with bands of electrical wire securely fastened at the deck level. Electrical current energizing these bands neutralizes the ship's magnetism. The *Esso Williamsburg* was so protected; it had been "degaussed."

Norfolk, Virginia on May 12: The ship is armed and equi
convoy. < See details in Chapter 5, The Navy Armed Guard>.
test fired at the Wolf Trap range in the Chesapeake Bay area. ᴛʜᴇ ᴊʜɪᴘ
departs Norfolk on May 14 en route to Houston, Texas to pick up oil.
She leaves Texas to make the run up the East Coast to New York.

On board is Pumpman Varise Mountain, 32-years-old, married
with two daughters. He's been on the ship a long time, living in Florida, sailing in yachts, making a living for his family. He's a tall guy,
almost six feet, and has a most demanding job on the *Esso Williamsburg*. He's the Pumpman.

He runs the ship's pumps to discharge oil from the ship to shore or to
some other ship, if need be. He has to have knowledge of all the valves and
internal pipes of the ship and how to discharge one tank after the other
and not stall out the pumps. When you discharge a ship, it is done one tank
after the other, turning one off (valve on deck) at the same time turning
one on, so to not lose the suction on the pumps. He works together with
one of the mates and several of the AB's. The Pumpman has got to have at
least an AB ticket, plus a lot of "hands on" experience. In wartime, when
the goal is to keep the oil moving, the Pumpman is invaluable in port, a
good one making the turnaround in the least amount of time. He's vital.

Letters provided by his daughters give a running account of what
life is like during these dangerous days.

We pick Varise up on the ship on May 23. He's writing to his wife, Mary:

M.S. Esso Williamsburg

At Sea

Dearest,

*Just a few lines this p.m. I don't know where we are going or
how long before we get there. I will call you from Baytown or
where we are going. We are in a 12 ship convoy. There was 13
but we lost one last night at 1:30 a.m. Here's hoping they don't
get us. Well bye for now. Love and Kisses, Varise*

At this point, ships are gathering around the Florida Straits to form
convoys that make the run up the coast to ports in the Northeastern
United States.

On May 25, Varise is off the West Coast of Florida:

Dearest,

At 10:00 a.m. we were off Egmont Key about 20 miles from you. I may as well have been 10,000 for all the good it done me. How is Patsy and Bobbie? Just fine, I hope. I have been working pretty hard lately. We will be . . . . Thursday a.m., so I will mail this then. I did not have such a good birthday this year, just another day. Well I will close for now and write more before we get in.

Love to all and a Happy Birthday to Patsy. Love, Daddy.

On May 27, he's writing again:

12:45 a.m.

Dear Mary, Patsy, and Bobbie,

I was awakened at 10:00 tonite and made to stand by. We will be in today about 6 p.m. I think. I passed 2 transports yesterday or rather Sunday in the Fla. Straits. They . . . .

Meanwhile, Dönitz is reporting that he is well aware of what the American tankers are doing:

American tankers instructed to anchor in DM 2710 (north of Key West) and await further orders. Boats <U-boats> were duly informed.

May 31, still at sea, Varise Mountain writes again:

We will be off Key West tonight and will probably pick up a convoy there. I sure hope so. We are going to Seacaucus, New Jersey. I guess we will be about the 6/9/42 as near as I can figure.

Oh yes the day we got into Baytown I wheeled to catch a governor on the cargo pump and cut my eye open and have got a nice black eye. I cut a gash about 1-1/4 inches long in my left eyebrow. But it is in good shape now. I had to see a doctor with it . . . .

This injury plagues Varise Mountain for the remainder of his time on the ship. He makes subsequent references to going to the hospital

in Aruba. It adds to his depression.

When the *Esso Williamsburg* arrives in New York with oil from Texas, two major personnel changes occur. The Mas Chief Mate are relieved. Captain John Tweed joins the ship .... Andreasen accepts the assignment as Chief Mate. Thus begins the last three months of their lives.

The ship is scheduled to sail from New York on June 17, 1942. According to documents issued by the Third Navy District in New York, it is designated to operate in "Area One, U.K." This represents a dramatic change from its previous schedule of coastal runs, and further explains why so much time was spent in May preparing the ship for wartime operation. On June 18, after sailing south from New York Harbor, the *Esso Williamsburg* arrives in Norfolk, Virginia. Here Communications Personnel, Navy Armed Guard Convoy Group, are assigned to the ship. "Personnel and equipment placed on board for convoy service (temporary)" is how it is presented.

From Norfolk, on June 20, the ship departs Lynnhaven Roads, Virginia for Baytown, Texas to fill up its tanks. Upon leaving Baytown on Wednesday, July 1, its destination is "bound for a point in the Atlantic." On Saturday July 11 (10 days into the voyage), Captain Tweed sends out the following wireless message via RCA Radiogram. Lea Maxwell Gayle, Jr., the ship's Radio Operator, relays the following message:

Broadcast on 16560 Kc.

To Admiralty de KVOF

267 degrees 170 position ZED 1200 GMT

11th July Master

At 1719 hours GMT on Tuesday, July 14, the ship received the following wireless message:

Fld. 1125/14

Alter course immediately for new position E. repetition E which is 6 degrees of longitude west of B repetition B fullstop thence direct to C repetition C.

Again the ship received instructions, this time on Wednesday, July 15:

Received at 0014 GMT July 15th from Gay-Portishead-S—Following for Esso Williamsburg PJAJ XLOP

Destination changed to Glasgow.

Next transmission occurs on Thursday, July 16th:

To GPK-Port Patrick

Sent 1836 GMT July 16th

Due destination 0500 GMT 17th July

They arrive in Glasgow Harbor at 7:30 a.m. on Friday, July 17, 1942. They have now about nine weeks left to live.

That Friday, Fred Kindl, Cox'n of the Navy Armed Guard, hand prints his "Report of trip from Baytown, Texas to Liverpool, destination was changed to Glasgow July 15":

Departed from Baytown, Texas Wednesday July 1st, l:30 p.m.; arrived in Glasgow 7:30 a.m. Friday July 17th. Nothing out of general routine occurred. Copies of messages attached. No conversations or observation took place in any foreign ports. Repairs for telephones. 15 knots was the average speed while in war zone.

He reports that the ship followed zigzagging instructions and that the Master and Officers carried out "Instructions for Navy Transportation and U. S. Merchant Vessels in Time of War."

Lt. Commander R. Miller of the USN Port Liaison Office, The Clyde, forwards Kindl's report on August 3 to The Chief of Navy Operations via the Commander. By August 18, the U. S. Navy Forces Europe in London has a copy of the report. 32 days elapse between Kindl's report and Navy's central headquarters receiving and reviewing it. This is how the process works for ships coming into Glasgow. Slow.

Not that they get to see much of wartime Glasgow. Merchant seamen are not allowed off their ships without permission of the Master. They are not allowed to converse with anyone in port, unless it is personnel related to ship's business. Glasgow is being subjected to many Luftwaffe raids. Houses and buildings are demolished or severely damaged. It's been like this for several years. At this point in time, the oil companies become exceedingly aware of what's called "turnaround time." How fast can a ship's tanks be emptied into the port tanks and prepared for the return voyage? In peacetime, turnaround is simply an economic matter. In wartime, it is strategic. Victory depends on getting as much oil as possible to the U.K. in the quickest manner.

In the summer of '42, Standard Oil begins its "Tanker Expediter Program," working with the War Shipping Administration, the U. S. Navy and the British Ministry of War Transport. Key personnel are sent to the United Kingdom, as well as thirteen other strategic areas, with one purpose in mind. They must minimize tanker time spent in discharge ports. Frequently these men work under very hazardous wartime conditions and in the U.K. they are particularly vulnerable to bombing raids.

The *Esso Williamsburg* gets in and out of Glasgow in record speed.

August 8: The ship sails back across the Atlantic and docks in Curacao to refill its tanks with the precious cargo so needed in the U.K.: oil. Varise Mountain sends a Postal Telegraph from Willemstad, the capital of Curacao, which simply says:

Greetings Love Varise Mountain

He sends an additional post card to Bobbie and Patsy:

Hello, do you want another monkey? If you do, be good girls and Daddie will bring you one or a parrot or something.

Love to you both, Daddie

On August 10, in Curacao NWI, Chief Engineer James F. Maher, Jr. joins the ship. As Chief Engineer, he is responsible for all the machinery on the ship. Since each ship is really a floating city, Maher's job is a big one. In the ship's last hours, his engines will prove to be critical.

Maher had been called to serve on the *Esso Williamsburg* abruptly. He'd traveled from Staten Island, NY to Miami, Florida to Willemstad, Curacao to pick up the ship. He had written a letter to his son, Frank, from the hotel in Miami:

Don't forget to say a little prayer each day for me. . . .

The clock is ticking and Chief Maher senses it. Somehow he seems to realize that he has only six weeks left of life.

The tanks are full. Once again alone, the *Esso Williamsburg* quietly slips out of the harbor at Willemstad and heads once again for the U.K., once again destined for Liverpool. They make it.

Meanwhile, the Tanker Expediter Program is in full swing in the U.K. Standard Oil has assigned three men to the United Kingdom, all of whom remain there until 1945. Andrew Thompson, Harry Marsh, and Clarence Marks are responsible for getting the ships unloaded and sent back to the U. S. as soon as humanly possible.

On August 23, the *Esso Williamsburg* sails into Liverpool Harbor.

Upon arriving, Fred Kindl, Navy Armed Guard Cox'n, submits his report. This one is more formal than the July report given in Glasgow. It's typewritten. This one, as retrieved from the U. S. Navy Armed Guard archives some fifty years later, is stamped "U. S. Secret British Most Secret."

He begins with a general resume of the voyage from Curacao to Liverpool. "Uneventful," he records. "No vessels or planes sighted during the voyage while in the open sea."

He goes on to describe the route the ship has taken to Liverpool:

We left Curacao, N.W.I. and proceeded to Atlantic Ocean by way of the Windward Islands and entered the waters of the British Islands by North side of Ireland and proceeded down the Irish Sea to Liverpool.

Regarding any items of general or special interest gathered in conversation or by observation in any foreign port, he relates "nothing observed." The speed of the ship in war zones is 15 to 16 knots. The vessel, he reports, followed zig-zag instructions and the Master and Officers of the ship carried out "Instructions for Navy Transportation and U. S. Merchant Vessels in Time of War." He types this up on Sunday, August 23.

Here it is necessary to look ahead to a memorandum sent by H. P. Swanton of the U. S. Navy Liaison Office in Liverpool dated September 6, 1942 to the Chief of Navy Operations. Paragraph 5 reads:

The master made a trip to London reporting by letter to Mr. B. B. Howard, Standard Oil Company. He was notified by

telegram sent by the agents, Furness-Withy, to return to Liver-
pool on Wednesday morning at 0900. He did not board his ship
until 1100 and then anchored in the Mersey to complete tank
cleaning before proceeding to sea. The ship was delayed in sail-
ing one day.

In light of the newly established "Tanker Expediter Program," it seems strange that the Master allows this to occur. This one day's delay will become critical to the safety of the *Esso Williamsburg* and her crew, as becomes apparent in September.

Many letters are written by the crew while in Liverpool. Henry (Buddie) Lehde is the 2nd Assistant Engineer. He is responsible for the fuel oil on board and the fresh water. The boilers are his job. The 2nd Assistant Engineer also usually stands the 12 to 4 watch, so Buddie is a busy guy.

His letter from Liverpool, dated August 27, 1942 is an eerie communication. When writing it at age 29, Buddie has 26 days left to live:

Liverpool, August 27, 1942

Dear Folks:

This is our second trip over since we left there. We were in Glasgow last trip. Don't know where we are going from here. Someplace in the (censored). There are quite a few fellows from Standard Oil over here. And as far as I can gather we won't be back in the states for six months. I sent some cards from Cura-cao. Hope you got them, haven't got any mail myself. Don't sup-pose they will send any to meet us this trip either . . .

So far we have been coming and going alone. They had an air raid warning here the other night and it like to scare us to death.

Have seen quite a few (censored).

Love, Buddie

On Thursday, August 27, they sail from Liverpool to Aruba, N.W.I. What happened on that voyage can best be told by Varise Mountain:

(Sunday) 8/30/42, At Sea

Dearest,

Just a word tonite as to events of this trip. We had an air raid the night of our arrival in England sure was some fun otherwise it has been an uneventful trip. This makes 2 ½ months since we were in the states don't know how much longer it will be before we get back. I guess about the 1st of the year.

I will be home in about 6 weeks. I will try to catch a plane from Aruba or a ship to New York but if I catch a plane it will go to Miami and then home to you and I am not going to sea any more.

Several things become apparent from this letter. First, the stay in Liverpool scares the men. In spite of the danger, they remain there an extra day, due to the Master's trip to London and his delayed return. Perhaps for the war beleaguered citizens of Liverpool the Luftwaffe bombing raids were "business as usual," but the men of the *Esso Williamsburg* have not been subjected to them before. Second, Mountain knows that the ship is going to operate outside of the U.S., at least until January of 1943. Then, he assures his wife that he will be home in "about six weeks." He evidently plans to make the run from Aruba to Iceland and back again, and then get off the ship. " . . . and I am not going to sea any more." Varise Mountain feels the danger, and decides to get out as soon as he can. But it gets worse.

On Monday, just three days out of Liverpool, he recounts the ultimate scare for those sailing on merchant ships in war zones.

(Monday) August 31st.

We had quite a scare last night. A sub surfaced off of our port stearn and asked us questions. I have still got the jitters. If I ever get back to the states I am sure going to stay there. I may get off in Aruba and catch a plane back. I don't know as yet I may go to the Hospital there. No more news for now so love and kisses to all. Varise.

That would be Sunday night, August 30. The event gives rise to several questions. Why would the sub stop the ship, instead of

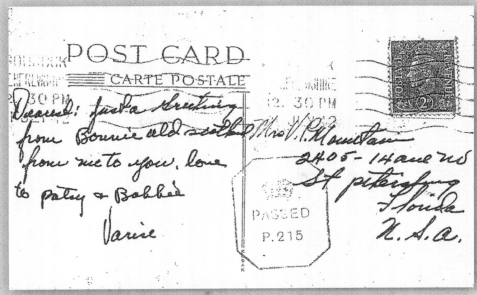

Varise Mountain Postcard from Scotland.
(Mountain Family)

Varise Mountain
Postcard from Curacao.
(Mountain Family)

Varise Mountain on Yacht. (Mountain Family)

2nd Assistant Engineer Henry F. Lehde
(Arthur Mohr)

Chief Engineer James F. Maher.
(Frank Maher)

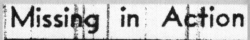

Missing in Action

FRED J. KINDL.

Cox'n Fred Kindl is reported missing.
(St. Louis Post—Dispatch)

sinking her? Because they were "in ballast," i.e., had no cargo? Perhaps the sub had used up her supply of torpedoes? What information were they seeking?

This, however, was the second turning point for Varise Mountain. His reference to the hospital in Aruba could relate to the injury he received in Baytown, or perhaps his nerves were just too shattered to go on. In retrospect, he surely should have gotten off the ship in Aruba.

On Thursday, September 10, the ship arrives in Oranjestad, Aruba. Chief Mate Hans Andreasen calls his wife at home on Staten Island, NY. He tells her a sub had chased them on the voyage from the U.K.

On September 12, her tanks filled with Navy fuel oil, the *Esso Williamsburg* leaves Aruba and sails off into oblivion.

CHAPTER TWO

MISSING

"On October 24, 1942, the War Shipping Administration reported the vessel and her crew long overdue and presumed lost as a result of enemy action."

Staten Island, some five by seven miles, sits at the entrance to New York Harbor, directly adjacent to New Jersey's industrial complex of oil refineries. Tall stacks belch fire and smoke night and day, creating serious air pollution problems. At dusk, the stacks create awesome sunsets, cruel combinations of the worst of science and the best of nature. At night the stacks glow, hugh golden eyes watching over the waters of the Kill Van Kull.

The island rests amidst this polluted nebula. Huge masses of smog hover over it. The sad wail of foghorns from ships in the Harbor and the Kill resonate. Long periods of carefully timed signals intersperse with dramatic short, staccato blasts that indicate near collisions.

Here I grew up.

I'm told that sometime in late September of 1942, at the age of four, I awakened one night, crying. In a dream, I saw my father on the burning deck of his ship as it sank.

Psychic? Perhaps.

Just as likely I drew on my sub-conscious, filled with overheard stories of ships that sank in the night, of the submarines that torpedoed them, of men in lifeboats for days and weeks on end, and of those who never came back. I eavesdropped while family friends visited our home and told stories of horror.

Did I, in my four-year-old mind, recreate these tales in my dream, making my father the protagonist? Or, did I receive a message on that night so long ago?

My father, Hans Didrik Andreasen, was Nordic of birth and Scandinavian in appearance. He was born on September 1, 1892 on Reksta Island, Norway off the coast and way out into the North Sea. Sailing in small boats on a huge sea was the way of life for the herring fisherman and their families who populated the island.

As an adult, he was fairly tall, 5'9", with blue eyes, a fair complexion, and auburn hair. On May 2, 1912 at the age of 20, he left home and the family fishing boats to sail as an ordinary seaman on the *S/S Marietta DiGiorgio*, a ship running between Bergen, Norway and New Orleans, Louisiana.

Two years later, on May 11, 1914 he signed off that ship in New Orleans and spent several years in Minneapolis living with relatives while getting his first American seagoing licenses.

Merchant shipping moved quickly from sail to steam, and he made the transition also, finding employment in American shipping companies and studying for his Mates' licenses as the years went by.

My father's story thus far is representative of the thousands of Scandinavians who immigrated into the United States in the early 1900's. Most seamen did not have the Ellis Island experience. Rather, they applied for citizenship at the port they found themselves in, when deciding to leave a ship.

Many joined the ranks of the United States Merchant Marine.

American merchant mariners became involved in World War II years before their country did. Beginning in 1939, Axis submarines hunted the waters of the Atlantic Ocean, the Caribbean Sea, and the Gulf of Mexico. Merchant ships were prime targets for these U-boats that would return home to German ports with pennants flying, one for each merchantman sunk. To avoid losing ships, many companies transferred their vessels to affiliates established in neutral countries. Panama was one of these. Several ships of the Standard Oil Company operated under the aegis of the Panama Shipping Company and, of course, flew the Panamanian flag. This flag, flown from a tanker's taffrail, was also painted on the superstructure to remove any doubt as to country of origin when seen through the periscope of a German U-boat.

Early in the year 1941, while employed by the Standard Oil Company, Hans Andreasen secured his first command, the *I. C. White*, a tanker owned by Panama Shipping and manned by an American crew. The ship's record was "excellent" during that time. In the summer of 1941, Captain Andreasen left that ship and came home on leave. In September of 1941, the *I. C. White* was torpedoed and sunk by an Axis submarine. The Panamanian flag did not protect it.

For most, this would have been a warning. He knew that men were burning to death on tankers attacked by U-boats, being cremated in flames and boiling oil both on deck and in the water, being sucked under by the pull of the sinking ship.

Merchant mariners, however, were drawn to danger by virtue of their trade. "Shipping out" was hard, hazardous work even in peaceful times. Wartime threats heightened risk, but risk was a way of life and, for many, it was addictive.

One of our neighbors was torpedoed early on in the war. Early memories are of my mother's friend, Alvilda Engelsen, stopping by our house in Westerleigh every day, particularly in those initial war years when wives of merchant mariners huddled like groups of frightened lemmings awaiting the next telegram.

The dreaded starred telegrams from the War Department arrived at random and without warning, a macabre lottery in which none knew whose number would be up next.

Alvilda was an early victim when her husband, Hans Engelsen, was torpedoed in December of 1940. What happened to Hans Engelsen on December 21, 1940 when he was Chief Mate on the *Charles Pratt* is a matter of public record. This occurred a full year before the entry of the United States into war with Germany. The *Pratt* sailed under the Panamanian flag as a neutral, supposedly protected from Axis submarine attack.

On 21 December 1940 U-65 attacked the *Charles Pratt*, a steam tanker sailing, alone, unarmed and under a neutral flag. She was en route from Aruba, NWI to Freetown, South Africa. The conflagration was so great that the crew abandoned her within twenty minutes. Hans Engelsen was thrown overboard by the blast, unconscious and with a broken leg.

Englesen was knocked unconscious by the torpedo's impact on the *Pratt*. He later recalled:

The next I knew I was in the ocean. Deep in the water. I came to, feeling a severe pain in my left side. I managed to swim to the surface and found myself about 50 feet astern of the ship, in a mass of oil.... Unable to find a piece of wreckage, I had to swim, mostly drifting and resting.

The captain of that ship recounted the rescue of Engelsen:

Finally we saw someone swimming. A few minutes later we had Chief Mate Engelsen in my lifeboat. He was completely covered with fuel oil and suffering from abrasions and cuts; his chest was injured and his left leg fractured.... From the time Mr. Engelsen went overboard until we picked him up, approximately 40 minutes had elapsed.

Engelsen went on to describe his rescue:

'I was in the bottom of the <life> boat,' he said, 'and unable to raise myself. Able Seaman Ralph Hansen sewed a piece of canvas around my chest. The upper part of my body was entirely covered with fuel oil. Hansen washed the oil out of my eyes with kerosene.'

The men were in a lifeboat for four days before being rescued. Even at that, they were lucky, because they *were* eventually saved.

Many men in lifeboats were left to die terrible deaths, sailing on endless oceans into nothingness.

Engelsen survived the sinking of the *Charles Pratt*, only to encounter a similar episode shortly after as Chief Mate onboard the *Esso Boston*, sunk on April 12, 1942 en route from Trinidad to Halifax, Nova Scotia. Once again he wound up in a lifeboat. This time, the men were in lifeboats for about 24 hours and were subsequently rescued by the *USS Biddle*, deposited in Puerto Rico by April 14, sailed for Tampa, FL on April 28, and arrived in New York by May 4, 1942. After a short leave they were sent out again into U-boat infested oceans, part of the deadly never-ending cycle.

Until the beginning of June, 1942 the two chiefs, Andreasen and Engelsen, lived within walking distance of one another's homes in Westerleigh. My father learned of Engelsen's four days in a lifeboat, while having crude petroleum washed out of his eyes with kerosene.

On the opposite side of Clove Lakes Park from Andreasen and Engelsen, in West Brighton, James Francis Maher, Jr. lived with his wife and three sons: Jim, Bill and Frankie. Maher began his career

with the Standard Oil Company in 1924 as a third assistant enginee
and had been promoted to Chief Engineer in June of 1939.

He was a well-seasoned marine engineer. In August of 1942, Maher received orders to join the *Esso Williamsburg* as Chief Engineer. He was to join the ship in Curacao and had to travel by train from his home on Staten Island to Miami and then on to Curacao. His son Frank, then five-years-old, remembers it this way:

> We went to Grand Central Station to see dad off. I was standing at the foot of that big marble staircase and he knelt down in front of me and up under his peaked cap he was crying. I thought that was strange for a sailor to do. He put his face close to mine and whispered, "You take good care of your mother— always." And then he was gone. It was years later that I realized he knew he wasn't coming back.

How did merchant mariners live in those days? Within hours of leaving home, these men were at sea making coastal runs and foreign voyages in submarine-plagued waters, upon oceans covered with oil. Some spent days and weeks in lifeboats, floating about like corks on an indifferent sea. Then, suddenly, they would be home again on short leaves, living in comparative peace. Then they shipped out again. That was the cycle.

The appalling stories they narrated of these voyages hung like huge dark clouds over their homes and families. Wives and mothers lived in fear. Who would be next in the macabre lottery? The men lived with the grim reality of a horrible death.

My father seemed fortunate, when he narrowly escaped death by virtue of having left the *I. C. White* just weeks before her sinking on September 27, 1941. First-hand information from Chief Mate Engelsen told him what it was like to be torpedoed and marooned in a lifeboat. And yet, in June of 1942 he left again. At this time, a Chief Mate was needed on the *Esso Williamsburg*, a 12,000 ton tanker owned by Standard Oil.

He didn't know that the *Esso Williamsburg* was a doomed ship. In June of '42, the clock of its destruction speedily ticked toward a frightful finish.

On October 27 of 1942, New York and Texas are the hardest hit states, when the Western Union delivery men are sent out with the five star telegrams from the U. S. Coast Guard.

n Island, a small borough of New York City located
w York Harbor and the Kill Van Kull, four families receive
ed telegram. From Westerleigh to West Brighton, from
к to New Brighton, four island families were about to be
dest. ed.

In Manhattan, the main borough of New York City, four more telegrams were about to be delivered. In the Bronx, another borough, one telegram was on the way. In yet another borough, Queens, another telegram was scheduled for delivery. And in Sayville, Long Island still another was on its way. Upstate New York, on Main Street in the small town of Nichols, another heart was about to be broken.

Texas took her share that day. All told, nine telegrams went out: Arlington, Hempstead, Navasota, El Paso, Willis, Galveston, Washington, Houston, and Baytown. From Harrington, Maine to San Pedro, California; from St. Louis, Missouri to St. Petersburg, Florida the message was going out.

The telegram, from Vice Admiral R. R. Waesche, Commandant of the United States Coast Guard, dated October 27, 1942 at 10:15 a.m. contained the following text:

> THE NAVY DEPARTMENT DEEPLY REGRETS TO INFORM YOU THAT YOUR (husband, son, brother, friend) (name of crew member) IS MISSING FOLLOWING ACTION IN THE PERFORMANCE OF HIS DUTY AND IN THE SERVICE OF HIS COUNTRY. THE COAST GUARD APPRECIATES YOUR GREAT ANXIETY AND WILL FURNISH YOU FURTHER INFORMATION PROMPTLY WHEN RECEIVED. TO PREVENT POSSIBLE AID TO OUR ENEMIES PLEASE DO NOT DIVULGE THE NAME OF HIS SHIP.

42 telegrams went out to next-of-kin of the crew members of the tanker *Esso Williamsburg*, en route on a voyage from Aruba, NWI to Iceland, carrying Navy fuel oil.

18 additional notifications were sent to families of the Navy Armed Guard stationed aboard the *Esso Williamsburg*. They, too, were listed as missing.

My mother remembered it this way. October 26, 1942 dawned like any other day. She was up early, getting her three girls ready for school. Baby Hans, six-months-old, was asleep in his crib. Shortly after 11 a.m., the doorbell rang. When she opened the door and saw a young man standing on the steps holding a star-emblazoned telegram, she knew that our family was a victim of the macabre lottery.

The Coast Guard appreciates your great anxiety and will furnish you further information promptly when received. <u>To prevent possible aid to our enemies please do not divulge the name of his ship.</u>

Since the next-of-kin were ordered by both the Government and the shipping companies not to divulge details of the ships and their voyages, grieving families had to fend off eager reporters from local and national newspapers. Another dilemma occurred in deciding whether or not the missing mariner was actually dead. How long did one wait, before losing hope? World War II for surviving family members of all 4,720 mariners reported "missing" was a time of ceaseless waiting.

In April of 1943, my mother received a letter from the U. S. Coast Guard (R. H. Farinholt <by direction PLGregg>), acknowledging her request for information on our father's fate.

To date no messages have been received from this vessel nor has any wreckage been found. I regret very much to advise the Navy Department has declared the vessel long overdue and presumed lost with all members of the crew, as a result of enemy action.

The letter went on to state:

The United States Coast Guard appreciates your deep anxiety in not having more definite information concerning your husband, and you may be assured we will notify you promptly if further information is received.

Beyond this, the United States Government never answered.

Service records of U. S. Merchant Mariners were maintained. In 1950, a little known volume was produced by the government.

A book entitled <u>Summary of Merchant Marine Personnel Casualties, World War II</u> was published by the U. S. Coast Guard on July 1, 1950. 845 men are listed as dead as a direct result of enemy action. Most astounding is that 4,780 men are listed as missing.

Almost a half century passed before the fate of the men on the *Esso Williamsburg,* and many of the thousands of other men categorized as missing, is revealed to their families.

Hans Didrik Andreasen (Andreasen Family)

CHAPTER THREE

SEARCH

What happened to the ship? Had it been attacked and sunk by a U-boat? Overcome by the horrendously bad weather conditions in the North Atlantic? Perhaps an accident on board led to their demise? None of these questions were answered. Like smoke rising from the stacks of a distant ship on a murky horizon, the *Esso Williamsburg* had just disappeared.

Interest stirred anew in 1988, when newspaper articles suggested that the government finally intended to recognize the merchant mariners who served so long and so heroically in World War II. Official status as veterans was their reward, after four decades of being overlooked and ignored. Although many saw such recognition as a victory, it must be seen in perspective. For example, if the average age of a merchant mariner in World War II was 30, these men should now be in their 70's, if indeed they were still alive. How much longer would the Government be required to give them benefits? Perhaps for five to ten more years? Of the approximately 5,500 merchant marine war casualties, how many of their widows survived to reap the benefit of a spouse's pension? Most likely, a minuscule number was still alive.

It is in the Mystic Seaport Museum Shop and Book Store in Mystic, Connecticut that I find the first clue to uncovering the fate of the *Esso Williamsburg*. Located in a loft over the Museum Shop, the Mystic Seaport Book Store comprises one of the best collections of maritime art, literature, non-fiction, and video and audiotapes in this country.

One particular volume is of interest: Jurgen Rohwer's <u>Axis Submarine Successes (1939-1942)</u>. First published in the English version by the United States Navy Institute Press in 1983, the book is an updated

ranslation of <u>Die U-Boot-Erfolge Der Achsenmachte 1939-1945</u>, originally published for the Bibliothek fur Aeitgeschichte by J. F. Lehmanns
Verlag, Munich, in 1968. This book contains information that aston-
ishes me.

In chronological order by date and hour, I see a listing of *every*
ship torpedoed and sunk by the Kriegsmarine in World War II.

The author provides several appendices, one an alphabetical listing of all ships sunk by Axis U-Boats. I found what I was looking for:
the *Esso Williamsburg*.

The entry read:

*23/0026 dt U-211 Hauser AK 7114 –T 10000+ T am   MT Esso
Williamsburg 11237+ 53/12N/ 41.00 W*

Using the Explanation of Table and Index Formats in the front of
the book for interpretation, a brief paraphrase recounts the fate of
the ship:

*On September 23, 1942 at 12:26 a.m. Greenwich Mean Time,
the German submarine U-211 commanded by KL Karl Hause in
grid AK 7114 (in the North Atlantic, roughly in the middle of
the Greenland Air Gap) targeted a tanker exceeding 10,000 tons
that was not identified but was reported sunk by torpedo. The
date of the first hit scored against the ship was September 22
with no specific time recorded. The nationality of the ship was
American, its type a motor tanker. The name of the ship, the
Esso Williamsburg, the actual tonnage (11,237 tons sunk), and
the position of the ship were determined "…according to data
of Allied authorities."*

Coincidence, chance, and twists of fate all played a recurring
part in determining the ship's destiny. Historian Clay Blair's <u>Hitler's
U-Boat War</u>, published in 1998 provides a comprehensive account
of the Kriegsmarine's record in World War II. Blair's narrative high-
lights what I came to realize was a sub-theme in the story of the *Esso
Williamsburg*: happenstance. "By happenstance, Hause in U-211
encountered the 11,200 American tanker Esso Williamsburg, which
was sailing alone, and sank her."

After online research in the U. S. National Archives and Records
Administration web site, I communicated by e-mail with the Civil Ref-

erence Staff at Archives II, College Park, MD. About six weeks later, a small box of microfilm arrived that contained:

Kriegstagebuch "U 211"

Kapitanleutnant Hause

Begonnen: 8 August 1942

Beendet: 7 Oktober 1942

Soon I am reading the entry for 21.9 (September 21):

1740 (5:40 p.m.) QU 6569 <Atlantic Ocean had been divided into quadrants for easy reference.> Tanker in Sicht. General-kurs 20 (degrees), 15 Sm, vorgesetzt. Weil Tanker Flagge fuhrt, durch FT Versenkungserlaubnis eingeholt und erhalten.

But what did this mean? Using Altavista for translation, I determine that U-211 radioed for permission to sink the ship. They did not know the name or nationality of the ship at that time. (N.B. Ships sunk were reported only in estimated tonnage to B-Dienst, the Nazi Navy intelligence/communications service. Frequently these estimates later proved to be exaggerated.)

Next, I enter in the German words of a subsequent entry on September 23. I understand this much: The ship lit up, a black mushroom of smoke rose, the masts leaned against one another, and the aft part separated and burned. The name of the ship was impossible to read. (N.B. Names of ships were obliterated because of wartime regulations.)

Another piece of the *Esso Williamsburg's* puzzle is found quite nearby, at the U. S. Merchant Marine Academy, Kings Point, New York. The Academy itself is unpretentious. Its prime location on the Gold Coast of Long Island Sound adds to its charm.

In their library I find Robert Browning, Jr.'s U. S. Merchant Vessel War Casualties of World War II, published by the Navy Institute Press in 1996. The volume reinforces Rohwer's version and also includes new information about the sinking of the *Esso Williamsburg.*

About 500 miles south of Cape Farewell, Greenland, the U-211 (Hauser) <sic> spotted the tanker and attacked. Two torpedoes *struck the tanker's port side. In poor visibility, the tanker got under way again and temporarily evaded the U-boat. The U-211 reportedly dove to use its listening gear to find the tanker.*

About ten hours later, the submarine again had the tanker in sight. From 2,000 yards, the U211 put a torpedo into the tanker's starboard side amidships, and Williamsburg caught fire. At 0105 the coup de grace shot struck amidships, and the smoke and flames from the explosion rose nearly 500 feet in the air. The tanker broke in two, and the after section continued to burn as both halves sank. The U-boat's war journal gave no mention of any of the eight officers, thirty-four men, and eighteen armed guards abandoning ship. It does, however, mention the ship sending a weak distress signal. A shore station received the message but an extensive air and sea search failed to find any survivors or wreckage. All hands perished in the attack.

This entry agrees with other versions of the sinking previously researched. The reference to an extensive air and sea search, however, was new.

Piece by piece, the story in the log unfolds. Eventually I locate a copy of the latest edition of <u>A Careless Word...A Needless Sinking</u>, written by a Captain Arthur Moore, who proves to be even more helpful later on in the search. A translation of excerpts from the log of the U-211 as provided in Captain Moore's book reveals the following scenario.

U-211 first encountered the *Esso Williamsburg* on Monday, September 21, 1942 at 3:40 p.m. GMT. (N.B. GMT is two hours earlier than the time used on the U-boats. Convoys operated on GMT.)

3:40 p.m., Monday September 21:

Tanker sighted on course of 020 degrees at a speed of 15 knots... Because the ship was flying a strange flag, the Commander radioed submarine headquarters to get permission to sink the tanker. This permission was obtained...In the meantime the sub proceeded to get ahead of the tanker.

Eight hours later, at 11:16 p.m., U-211 catches up with the tanker:

A two torpedo spread was fired. Two hits were heard in the sub. The tanker was seen to stop. At this time the visibility became very poor. When it cleared, the tanker was nowhere to be seen. At this time the U-211 submerged to use the underwater listening apparatus. The tanker could be heard but still could not be seen. According to the sound bearing, the tanker was still moving about 10 knots.

Questions come to mind. Was the crew of the *Esso Williamsburg* aware that they had been sighted on the afternoon of the 21st? Were they trying to outrun the U-211? And after eight hours, when they were finally caught in the crosshairs of the periscope, how badly was the ship damaged by the two torpedoes? Was the damage minimal, since in that seemingly blessed fog they were still able to sail, even if at only 10 knots? Or were they carrying one or two torpedoes in the ship? And what about that cargo of Navy fuel? Was the ship on fire even then?

Ten hours later at 9:19 a.m. on Tuesday, September 22:

Tanker is sighted. Sub proceeds at full speed to get ahead of the ship. Position 50-51 N/39-45 W.

Thirteen hours later at 10:26 p.m. on September 22, U-211 again catches up with the ship:

A single torpedo fired which struck the tanker amidships. After a violent explosion, a hugh black column of smoke rose from the ship and the midship house burned brightly.

Ten minutes later, another entry was made:

Another torpedo fired from stern tube which missed. At this time a radio message was heard coming from the tanker on a 600 meter frequency with very low volume which denoted the transmitter was broken or the antenna was down. Garbled Morse signals were heard and it was not possible to determine the name of the tanker.

Could this have been a signal from a lifeboat? Did the tanker's crew use the ten minutes between the first torpedo and the second to escape? By this point, the U-211 had used four torpedoes on the tanker.

Again ten minutes later, at 10:46 p.m.:

There was another explosion aboard the tanker spreading the fire to the after house. The ship had a severe list to starboard.

Nineteen minutes later, at 11:05 p.m.:

In position 52-45 N/39-45 W: Another torpedo fired which hit on the starboard side amidships which caused the entire ship to light up in flames. A black column of smoke rose for a height of 300 feet above the ship. The masts of the ship then commenced to tilt toward each other and the ship broke in two and the two parts floated free from each other. The after part still burned. Impossible to read the ship's name on the bow or stern. The funnel was black with no marking. An empty liferaft was seen without marking.

Fifty-five minutes later, at 12:00 midnight:

U-211 left the scene with the tanker still sinking. The sub commander estimated the ship at 10,000 tons. (In the log he describes the ship's armament and the ship was painted gray. Nowhere in the log was there any mention of survivors.)

From the first attack on the evening of Monday, September 21 at 11:16 p.m. when the first torpedoes were fired, until midnight of Tuesday, September 22 when the U-211 left the scene, the *Esso Williamsburg* had been under attack for more than 24 hours and had been hit with a total of four torpedoes, a fifth having missed the mark. The distance run between attacks was about 114 nautical miles.

Kriegstagebuch

"U 211"

Kapitänleutnant   H a u s e . .

Begonnen: 8. August 1942.

Beendet: 7. Oktober 1942.

mit 1 Wege karte

Official Log of U-211. (US National Archives)

	Qu .... trübe	
	.... Licht	
0600	Qu 6957.	
1200	Qu 6943, NO 1, ein-	
	zelne Wolken, diesig,	
	Nebelschwaden......	

Etmal: ∠ 157 Sm.
6 Sm.

BC

1600	Qu 6743, NO 1, aufge-	Marsch zum Vorpostenstreifen von Qu BC 3143
	klärt, gute Sicht	bis 3851 angetreten. (FT 1047/21/258).
1740	Qu 6569.	Tanker in Sicht. Generalkurs 20°, 15 Sm, vor-
		gesetzt. Weil Tanker Flagge führt, durch FT
		Versenkungserlaubnis eingeholt und erhalten.
		(1908/21/275 und 2010/21/276).

2000	Qu 6613, NO 1, leicht	
	bedeckt, diesig,	
	mässige Sicht.	
2400	Qu 6312	

Hansen.....

22.9.

0116	Qu BC 3971, NO 1,	Zweierfächer. Eingestellte Gegnerfahrt 15,
	geringe Dünung, trübe,	Lage 90, E 25. xxxxxxxxxxxxxxxxxxxxxxxxx
	Nebelschwaden, dun-	2 Treffer in Boot und auf der Brücke gehört.
	kel.	Tanker stoppte, weiter keine Wirkung zu be-
		obachten. In plötzlich xx besonders starke
		Sichtverschlechterung muß Tanker mit Fahrt
		gegangen sein. Längere Zeit aus Sicht. Mehr-
		mals getaucht zum Horchen, immer in der Nä-
		gehört, aber nicht in Sicht bekommen. Nach
		Horchpeilung lief er noch über 10 Sm.
0400	Qu BC 3914	Zeitweise nur klar für 12 Sm, da Geblüsekup-
0800	Qu 3615	lung Stb.-Diesel mehrmals rutschte.
1119		Tanker wieder in Sicht (recht voraus). Mit
		AK vorgesetzt.
1200	Qu 3315, NNO 5,	
	See 4, mässige Sicht.	Etmal: ∠ 315 Sm.
		2 Sm.
1600	Qu AK 7712, NNO 5,	
	See 4, 1020 mb, leicht	
	bedeckt, mittlere	
	Sicht.	
2000	Qu 7412	
2400	Qu 7114	

Hansen...

U-211 Log description of attack on *Esso Williamsburg*. (US National Archives)

CHAPTER FOUR

CREW

Solving the mystery of the *Esso Williamsburg's* disappearance is apparently at an end, but the search for the families of the 59 other crew members is just beginning. For the last several years, attempts at finding information on surviving family members of the crew have been unsuccessful, their identities obscured by time. Were it not for the advent of the Internet, some surviving family members would never have been found.

It begins in Houston, a city in Southeastern Texas, a humid metropolis that is corporate headquarters for the powerful oil industry. Less than an hour's drive south of the city are the ports of call so familiar to tankermen and their families: Baytown and Galveston. Here huge refineries churn out the products that run the economy and the war. Here tankers swallow vast quantities of crude and refined oil and race off to all parts of the globe with their precious cargo.

It's not so surprising, then, that many Texans become mariners. Opportunity to ship out to ports around the world abounds.

In times of war, these opportunities are deadly. So it was for Henry F. (Buddie) Lehde, 2nd Assistant Engineer on the *Esso Williamsburg.*

From: mohr@myriad.net (Arthur Mohr)

To: normaandre@aol.com

Dear Norma Andreasen,

*I write as a result of reading your query on the internet mention-
ing the Esso Williamsburg on which your father Hans Andreasen
was lost. Henry F. (Buddie) Lehde, my uncle was 2nd Assistant
Engineer on this ship. I know next to nothing about the ship or
circumstances or location of the loss of this ship and was interested in your saying it was in the Greenland gap. Of course, I
would like to know more! Have you identified the U-boat which
torpedoed this tanker?*

*I remember hearing about Aruba, Bayonne and Baytown as
ports this ship visited prior to the war, but during the war, due to
censorship etc. there isn't much that I can recall being discussed
within the family.*

*Buddie has two sisters who survive who may have some infor-
mation. I recall that one aunt has several items of furniture
from an apartment that Buddie had in the NYC area--these
items were delivered to her by a former shipmate of his whose
name I can't recall.*

*I have a copy of a censored letter from Buddie of August 27,
1942 from Liverpool in which he said the previous trip over was
to Glasgow, that he sent some cards from Curacao, that they
had an air raid warning the other night which scared him to
death--have seen quite a few (word censored).*

*Should you have comments or questions, I would be most happy
to hear from you and will pass it on to these two Aunts.*

*Sincerely,
Arthur Mohr*

**Surfing the Internet prior to receiving Arthur Mohr's inquiry
revealed a web site run by Dan and Toni Horodysky: www.usmm.org.
One of the many pages in this site, dedicated to merchant mariners
who gave their lives in all wars, is the Shipmate Search page. Posted
inquiries lead to connections with old buddies or provide information
on ships, voyages, and crews of the past. Several months *before* receiv-**

ing the e-mail from Art Mohr, the following inquiry was posted at my request on Shipmate Search, courtesy of Dan and Toni Horodysky:

Esso Fleet in WWII

SS Esso Williamsburg

SS I. C. White

SS F. G. Barstow

Hans D. Andreasen

My father, Hans D. Andreasen, was on board as Chief Mate of the SS Esso Williamsburg when it was torpedoed in the Greenland Air Gap in September of 1942.

All hands on the Esso Williamsburg were lost. He was also wartime master of the I. C. White, and sailed on the F. G. Barstow in the early months of the war. I am, however, interested in hearing from any surviving family members of the crew/Navy guard, as well as from shipmates who sailed with him on other vessels of the Esso fleet during WWII. I also have an interest in hearing from surviving family members of Esso tankermen who lived in the Staten Island/Brooklyn, New York area during the war.

Norma Andreasen

normaandre@aol.com

Through the Shipmate Search and Art Mohr, the story of Buddie Lehde, 2nd Assistant Engineer on the *Esso Williamsburg,* is discovered. Buddie was born in Washington, Texas, within a few hours drive of Houston, on July 2, 1913. Buddie grew up in a large two-storied house with a columned portico and chimneys at either end, set on prairie grass, surrounded by huge trees. He attended Brown's Prairie School, Navasota High School, and Texas A & M College. When confirmed at the Friedens Evangelical Church in 1929, Buddie chose a passage from Psalms as his memory verse: "Commit thy way unto Jehovah; trust also in Him and He will bring it to pass."

In the late 1930's, Buddie got a seagoing job with the Standard Oil Company. Photos of him on the deck of the tanker *John Archbold* show a handsome young man, well-groomed, with neatly combed dark hair, high cheekbones, and an impish grin. He is surrounded by his sister, Hilma, and sister-in-law, Alice, who wear middy dresses that blow in a wind that sweeps across the deck. Buddie is in work clothes: dungarees and a short-sleeved shirt that is open at the neck. He has the bronzed complexion of those who go to sea.

Buddie's father, Henry C. Lehde, was listed as his next-of-kin. As such, he received the starred telegram that declared Buddie as "missing at sea." Art Mohr writes, "Being flatlanders and knowing little of the sea or the life of seamen, we had no experience or context to fit the news...that Buddie was lost at sea. My mother wanted to believe that he would return at war's end—that perhaps he was a POW."

Buddie's sister, Emma, remembers that last summer of '42 this way. "The *Williamsburg* took on high octane fuel at Aruba and was shadowed by an Italian sub after leaving...was at berth in Baytown for about a week.

During this week, Buddie, along with Eric (his brother) and Alice visited relatives. Buddie reassured his kin saying, "There is nothing to worry about, there are 17 guns on board and besides, the *Esso Williamsburg* can outrun the submarines."

In September of 1944, Henry C. Lehde received his son's Mariner's Medal, the purple heart of the U. S. Merchant Marines, at a special memorial service in Washington, Texas. Within the week, Buddie's dad passed away.

In January of 1999, Art Mohr begins discussing via e-mail the possibility of finding other surviving family members. The recently discovered <u>Summary of Merchant Marine Personnel Casualties, World War II</u>, published by the U. S. Coast Guard on July 1, 1950, contains a list of men killed and missing, as well as their home addresses and persons designated as next-of-kin.

Previously, Art had inquired:

A possibility perhaps—that list of crew members if it has names of seamen from Baytown or environs may be the key to finding other survivors. That is something that I could pursue with an 82-year-old cousin who made half a voyage working on the same ship as Buddie.

The book provides the names of crew members from the Texas area. Art's investigation reveals relatives of Cecil Cloyd, another member of the crew.

I will be checking on Seaman Cecil Cloyd with the Hempstead <Texas> first of kin. Hempstead is near <Art was in College Station>, small and I know an elderly person who grew up there. I know that persons with the Cloyd surname live in Bellville which is 15-20 miles from Hempstead.

Art locates Cecil Cloyd, Jr. in Iowa:

It was much quicker and easier than I had ever imagined. My second telephone call resulted in speaking with Raymond Cloyd, a 73-year-old nephew of Cecil Cloyd. Cecil has a surviving son....

On January 30, 1999 Art phones Cecil Cloyd, Jr. After relating to Cecil the information gathered on the fate of the ship and its men, Art reports:

Both Cecil and Donna <his wife> were on the phone...saying my call made his day.

Cecil Cloyd, Jr.'s daughter, Katrina Wenger, e-mails shortly after. Her message provides insight into the varied backgrounds of the men on the ship, this fellow coming from Oklahoma to sail on merchant vessels:

My father was nine years old when his father went into the Merchant Marines....His dad came to see him the middle of May 1942 in Woodward, Oklahoma. My father's birthday is May 23rd and he was with him the week before. They took him to the train station to go to Topeka to join the Merchant Marines. As he waved good-bye, when the train pulled out of the station, was the last time he saw his father.

A note received later on from Katrina Wenger reveals that recognition for the men of the *Esso Williamsburg* was finally beginning:

I hope this finds you and your family all doing fine. I finally ordered the medals that were due my grandfather. I ordered them when I was in Iowa so that Dad would get them there. He received them a couple weeks ago. I won't get to see them until I go back to Iowa. I want to say that we appreciate the help that you have given us for getting these. It was important for Dad to get the medals before something happens to him.

In addition to the Mariner's Medal, awarded posthumously to next-of-kin, each crew member of the *Esso Williamsburg* earned the Atlantic War Zone Medal, the Merchant Marine Combat Bar with Battle Star, and the Victory Medal for WWII. Little by little, their surviving relatives step forward to claim the awards.

The next of Art Mohr's research achievements involves Fred McLee Jones. Art discovers an e-mail address for Armond Jones, a nephew of Fred McLee, who lives a short distance away in Conroe, Texas. Art shares the news:

Mr. Jones writes: "Thanks for your e-mail last week. It is amazing after so many years to find out what happened to the Williamsburg and <that> our uncles were shipmates. How I wish my father would have known this before his death.

Soon after I receive an e-mail from Armond Jones. His message expresses perfectly in human terms the loss resulting from the sinking of the *Esso Williamsburg:*

My father's brother who was 19 years old in 1942 went aboard this ship either at Beaumont, TX. Or Galveston TX. In May 1942. His last letter to his parents was dated Aug. 26, 1942 from Liverpool, England. He was a messman on this ship. He was lost forever at a young age, so long ago, never to enjoy a wife or children. What a waste. Anyway all of that family are dead now and I am the only one left who remembers him. I have his Mariners Medal and press clippings. I saw your letter on the net and do not know if this information would be of any interest to you. If so, let me know. By the way his name was Fred McLee Jones.

Slowly, the crew of the *Esso Williamsburg* comes alive again through such communications.

Meanwhile, Art Mohr is on the trail of Lea Gayle, Jr., radioman on the *Williamsburg*, and sends an encouraging message:

I had a telephone conversation with Charlotte Beth (Simons) Work-man, a cousin one generation younger than Lea, Jr. She remembered the mariner, but suggested I talk with 90-year-old Milam Travis Simons who remembers even better. There is nothing that he could add from Lea's letters or such. Lea did not know or did not reveal the destination of the next voyage. Milam Travis suspected that he was bound for Russia. He mentioned that Lea's aunt had a memorial stone/marker placed in the Edna, Texas Cemetery for Lea, Jr.

Shortly after, Art and his wife, Ann, find the history associated with Lea Gayle:

Ann and I checked on Lea Gayle, Jr. while in Edna <Texas> recently. His Gayle ancestors came to Texas from Virginia before statehood in 1835. His ancestors are noted in the fight for Texas independence. Our mission was to observe the Lea Jr. memorial stone which we found. It is a replica of his father's stone which it is adjacent to. It appears as a grave marker, however it does have 'lost at sea 1943' on it.

A number of Lea's relatives still live in Edna. One with whom we spoke is an 84 year old first cousin who with her Daughters of the Republic of Texas sisters are much interested in the story that you've researched. 90ish Milam Travis Simons, my first Lea Gayle contact, apparently has not shared any of the story. (He did say his vision prevented him from reading.) Milam and Travis are heroes of the Texas Revolution.

And so another hero joined this intrepid Gayle family of Texas Revolution fame: Lea Gayle, Jr., almost 26-years-old at the time of the *Esso Williamsburg's* sinking.

Later on in 1999, Art Mohr makes another "find." He e-mails:

Varise P. Mountain: This Esso Williamsburg mariner is survived by two sisters and two daughters! This information comes from Frasier Mountain of Brooksville, Florida.... Both daughters are in

Florida and one does have e-mail.... Frasier (76) is a first cousin of Varise Patton Mountain. He used the exact same phrase as did Cecil Cloyd which was, you have made my day. The Mountain family did not know any of the details of your story.

Before long, Bobbie Mosher, daughter of Varise Mountain, emails:

Norma,

My Father was Varise P. Mountain and I have an older sister, Pattie. Around 1993, Pattie requested the Mariner's Medal from the V.A. and happened also to receive an index page that gave an account of the German ship that had torpedoed our father's ship. Our mother died Jan. 24, l988 and she did not know that the date of 1/19/88 gave merchant seaman veteran's status...and she would have been eligible for V.A. benefits. Just this past November I received the Mariner's Medal from the V.A. along with a certificate showing my father served in the U. S. Coast Guard. I've met very few people that have known my father. Thank you so much for this opportunity. I hope to hear from you.

Bobbie Mosher

Varise Mountain was a loving husband and father. Bobbie shares several poignant postcards from Varise written during the summer of 1942. The first, postmarked in July and addressed to Bobbie's mother, Mary, reads:

Dearest, Just a greeting from Bonnie Old Scotland from me to you. Love to Patsy and Bobbie.

Varise

Next, Varise mailed a card dated August 10 from Curacao addressed to Mary Mountain :

Dearest:

Just a word as everything is censored so much to let you know I am safe. Will see you when I get back. Love to Patsy and

Bobbie. Had a nice trip and hope to see you soon about October 1. Love and kisses.

Varise

A third and last card was postmarked September 11, ten days before the first attack of the U-211 on the *Esso Williamsburg,* from Oranjestad, Aruba and addressed to Patsy and Bobbie. They received this final communiqué from their father *after* the telegram that reported him missing, a message in a sense from another world.

A photograph enclosed with copies of the postcards shows a monument in St. Petersburg, Florida:

Dedicated to the memory of merchant seamen of this community who in World War II gave their lives in the service of their country.

Varise P. Mountain is one of the eleven men listed.

In Nova Scotia, Canada on Cape Breton Island, which juts out into the Atlantic Ocean, is the village of St. Peters. This seafaring village was originally called Saint Pierre by early French settlers. Stunning sunrises and sunsets attract tourists, who arrive by car, bus, or ferry to enjoy the quaint inns and shellfish delicacies. Its population today is less than 3,000.

In this village stands a cenotaph, a memorial plaque to community members who lost their lives in World War II. One name puzzles a fellow named Don Pottie, who lives up there. *Frederick Boucher.*

Who was he? How did he die? No one seems to know. The inscription reads: *Erected in grateful memory to the men of St. John the Baptist parish who faithfully served in two world wars. These made the supreme sacrifice.*

In Long Island, New York Matty Loughran, Historian of the American Association of American Merchant Marine Veterans (North Atlantic Chapter), receives an inquiry from Don Pottie.

Matty is "out there" on the web and has been for quite some time. His quest is a simple one: To help as many former merchant mariners and their families as he can. Matty researches, emails, and gets people together to help find answers to the many mysteries of World War II and American merchant mariners.

So when Don Pottie asks Matty about "Fredrick Boucher," Mattie finds the name on the list of missing mariners of the *Esso Williamsburg*. And I am Matty's contact on that ship.

Don has since located Leo Bouchie, learns the following, and emails the information:

Frederick has only two surviving family members, a niece and a nephew. They knew very little of what happened to their uncle, only that he served on an American merchant ship and he was lost during the war. Fredrick's nephew tells me that he remembers his family being told very little, but that they should not repeat whatever was told to them.

The recurring secrecy theme: families told not to speak about their loved one's demise. The fog of war. Fear of aiding and abetting the enemy. Loose lips sink ships. For merchant mariners, whose ships were being sunk by the hundreds in 1942-43, denial that the war at that point was being lost became a mantra. How would the government attract more men to the merchant marine, if the truth were told?

I share with Don Pottie what I know of Fred S. Boucher. Fred was on the crew list as of June of 1942, listed as being born in Britain. He was employed as an Ablebodied Seaman. At the time of his coming aboard the *Esso Williamsburg*, he was 51-years-old. He was 5' 5" tall and lived in Arlington, Massachusetts with his wife, Artemes. Soon a letter arrives from his nephew, Leo Bouchie (the French spelling of Boucher).

I was very young the last time I saw Uncle Freddie. It was in 1939. He and a friend came to visit us and had dinner at our house. He had immigrated to the USA in the late 1920's/ early 30's. I was a child of six then and he gave me fifty cents American money. 50 cents was a lot of money for children in 1939. A bad depression was in effect and our family was poor, but through it all we had a small farm, a strong devotion for one another, and from my mother and dad's work we all survived.

He tells how the family learns of Frederick's death.

We were informed of Uncle Fred's death but the details were "skimpy." Wartime regulations, etc. My mother always thought the death had taken place around the Hebrides. We did not really know. We knew it was an American tanker, but we did not know which one until you verified it. Without your effort in doing this research, we wouldn't have known.

Thus it is that the mystery man of St. Peters cenotaph, Frederick Boucher, is given his place in history. More stories come to light over the years.

Junior Engineer Hobart Richards was 26-years-old at the time of the sinking. He was from Houston, Texas. His mother, Mrs. Edith Allen, and his sister, Mrs. J. C. Pinkerton survived him, as well as his brother, Sidney, who was a U. S. Marine stationed in the Solomon Islands at the time of Hobart's death.

William S. Teague, born in New Jersey, was on board as a wiper, one of the entry level positions. He was only 20 years of age, when he died. His sister, Carole Condon, wrote:

My brother, William S. Teague was lost 9/23/42 on the Williamsburg. I was only a year old and never knew him, only the memories of devastated parents and family members. He was bound and determined to serve his country. I'm not sure, but I think he was reported missing after only 6 months or so.

Lt. Colonel Kenneth J. Vennell of the Illinois Air National Guard wrote that his uncle Clarence was on board the *Esso Williamsburg* on that last trip. "My dad never knew the name of the ship, only that it was an Esso and was sunk by a torpedo."

More than fifty years after their deaths, the men of the *Esso Williamsburg* emerge. As it slowly unfolds, the story of the *Esso Williamsburg* proves to be in microcosm the plight of those who served in the United States Merchant Marine in World War II.

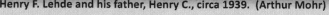

Henry F. Lehde and his father, Henry C., circa 1939. (Arthur Mohr)

Radio Operator Lea M. Gayle. (Arthur Mohr)

AB Fred Boucher of Nova Scotia.
(Leo Bouchie and Don Pottie)

1914
1918

1939
1945

ERECTED IN GRATEFUL
MEMORY TO THE MEN OF
ST. JOHN THE BAPTIST PARISH
WHO FAITHFULLY SERVED
IN TWO WORLD WARS
THESE MADE THE
SUPREME SACRIFICE

DOUGLAS BOURQUE
HERMAN MacNEIL
JOSEPH SAMSON
AUGUSTINE BOURQUE
ABRAHAM BOURQUE
EDMUND SAMSON
MARK SAMSON
SAMUEL PATE
WALTER PATE
MARTIN SAMSON
FREDERICK BOUCHER

World War II cenotaph memorializing Fred Boucher at St. Peters, Nova Scotia. (Leo Bouchie and Don Pottie)

Junior Engineer Hobart H. Richards. (Arthur Mohr)

CHAPTER FIVE

THE U. S. NAVY ARMED GUARD

Little known to those outside the maritime community is the plight of the U. S. Navy Armed Guard in World War II.

Once boot camp was completed, young Navy recruits were sent to man guns hastily being installed on American merchant vessels. In retrospect, the idea that arming merchant ships could in any way present a threat to Hitler's U-boat initiative seems ludicrous. But, at the time, placing guns and Navy Armed Guard crews aboard these ships created the illusion of protection.

Even more bizarre was the treatment of the Navy Armed Guard by the Navy itself.

These young men stumbled into the arms of war against a deadly enemy who knew no mercy. Eighteen of these unfortunate young men were aboard the ill-fated *Esso Williamsburg*. Records of this group received from the National Archives reveal much about the ship and its crew.

To begin with, a confidential memorandum dated June 2, 1943, written by Lieutenant (jg) Joseph B. Higgs, indicates by handwritten addendum that the *Esso Williamsburg* was sunk on September 24, 1942 "by surface craft." This, of course, proves to be untrue and typifies the confusion that existed during WW II as to merchant vessels and enemy attacks.

Other documents are more helpful in sketching out the ship and its preparation for war. One PORT DIRECTOR'S REPORT ARMING MERCHANT VESSELS gives an itinerary for the ship with a sailing date of May 14, 1942 from Norfolk, Virginia to Houston, Texas. The Master then is Peder A. Johnson. Nine men are listed as U. S. Navy Personnel, all in the United States Navy Reserve:

Kindl, Fred John   Coxwain

Goodrich, Moses A.S. V-6

Gaddy, Reuben R. A.S. V-6

Griffith, Doyle W. A.S. V-6

Hamburg, Leo J.   A.S. V-6

Glover, Robert L.   A.S. V-6

Greenwell, John   A.S. V-6

Glover, Stephen F. A.S. V-6

Hicks, Bruce O.   A.S. V-6

On a similar report from the Newport News, Virginia shipyard, the number and type of armaments installed on the *Esso Williamsburg* include:

1   3" .23 Cal.   Located Forward

1   5" .51 Cal.   Located Aft

1   .50 Cal. B.M.G. Aft & Starboard

2   .30 Cal. B.M.G. Bridge Port & Starboard

Added to this unimpressive collection are one .45 caliber pistol with 240 rounds, and 4 Colt .45 pistols. The ship is given one coat of gray paint.

Other equipment includes 43 "and other old type" Navy Life Jackets, 4 Life Rafts (capacity 18 per raft), and 4 Life Boats with emergency rations. Among the "Moveable Equipment Issued to Armed Guard

Unit" is "Special Submarine Clothing": 10 Coats, balloon cloth; 10 Trousers, balloon cloth; 10 Coats, woolen; and 10 Trousers, woolen.

One Welfare and Recreational Outfit is included. Someone had a sense of humor.

In an earlier (probably May of 1942) PORT DIRECTOR'S REPORT ARMING MERCHANT VESSELS from Newport News lists 24 Navy-type Life Jackets, 4 Life Rafts, and 2 Life Boats (40 persons each). When the *Esso Williamsburg* arrives in New York on June 18, 1942, four additional men are put aboard:

Reaves, Iris Vernon	A.S., V-6	USNR
Mayhew, Marle N.	S2/c. V-6	USNR
Byrd, Walter, Jr.	S2/c. V-6	USNR
Bryant, Donald Adair	S2/c. V-6	USNR

A separate group listed as Communication Liaison Personnel also joins the ship on this date:

Matecki, Jack R.	SM2/c. V-6 USNR	
Morrell, Joseph M.	S2/c. V-6	USNR
Cannon, Carl (n) <sic>	S2/c. V-6	USNR
Johnson, Alfred J.	S2/c. V-6	USNR

Yet, these four men are *not* aboard the *Esso Williamsburg* on her final voyage to Iceland and did not perish with the ship and its crew. Why were they placed aboard on June 18, when this ship was making unescorted runs to and from the U. K.? Why were they removed before the trip from Aruba to Reykjavik? The top speed of the *Esso Williamsburg* was much faster than that of the average convoy. Perhaps it was judged that she had a better chance making lone voyages?

To continue, twelve rockets, white (for Armed Guard) are furnished by the Bureau of Ordnance at this port, as well as 24 rounds of ammunition for one very pistol (red) and one very pistol (green).

One T.B.Y. radio telephone set, one 8-inch signal searchlight, one set of convoy colored lights, one set of international signal flags ("E", "Z", and "I"), one black square pennant 7.25 x 7.25, and one #6 pennant, large size were included with the notation that "Personnel and equipment placed on board for convoy service (temporary)."

So goes the preparation of merchant vessels for service in enemy waters in 1942.

From the Navy Armed Guard files two significant facts come to light that may or may not have contributed to the ultimate fate of the *Esso Williamsburg.* Both are found in a document stamped "U. S. Secret – British Most Secret," in the form of a memorandum dated September 6, 1942 written by H. P. Swanton, the U. S. Navy Liaison Officer, Liverpool, England to the Chief of Navy Operations. The subject is the *Esso Williamsburg's* voyage that culminated in Liverpool on August 24, 1942. In addition to information on testing of compasses and degaussing, two items are noteworthy:

> *3. The ship has the proper radio equipment but the high frequency transmitter was not adjusted to proper convoy frequencies. The agents were instructed to have this condition corrected.*

Here one is tempted to wonder about the radio message that was heard coming from the tanker on the 600 meter frequency as reported in the U-211's log. Was the "very low volume which denoted the transmitter was broken or the antenna was down and the garbled Morse signals" the result of damage from the attack, or from improperly adjusted radio equipment? The second item is even more fascinating, as previously noted:

> *5. The master made a trip to London reporting by letter to Mr. B. B. Howard, Standard Oil of New Jersey. He was notified by telegram sent by the agents Furness-Withy, to return to Liverpool on Wednesday morning at 0900. He did not board his ship until 1100 and then anchored in the Mersey to complete tank cleaning before proceeding to sea. The ship was delayed in sailing one day.*

In light of wartime conditions, it seems strange that the master made this overland trip. Certainly travel from Liverpool to London must have been hazardous in and of itself. The distance between Liverpool and London is approximately 176 miles. Driving distance today is about 212 miles, almost a four hour drive. Back in 1942, travel time must have been considerably longer. Wartime conditions and slower modes of transportation both would have contributed to the duration of the trip.

Had he noticed something awry on the voyage to Liverpool? Fred Kindl had written in his report of the voyage: "Uneventful. No vessels or planes sighted during the voyage while in the open sea." He went on to state that nothing of interest was gathered in conversation or observation in any foreign port.

The ship was sailing under the auspices of the War Shipping Administration. Why would Capt. Tweed have sent a letter to B. B. Howard, who was the General Manager of the Marine Department of Standard Oil? Whatever the reason was for the trip, the agents Furness-Withy ordered him back to Liverpool post haste.

What leads to further speculation is that the ship, as a result of the delay, arrives one day later than scheduled in Aruba. It does seem plausible that it then left Aruba one day later. Once again, the theme of "happenstance" works its way into the story of the *Esso Williamsburg's* disaster. If the ship had sailed for Reykjavik one day earlier, it would not have crossed paths with the U-211.

Delving further into the Navy Armed Guard records, I found a report written by A. C. Veasey, The Commander, U. S. Navy Forces in Europe, to the Chief of Navy Operations, dated September 9, 1942, once again stamped "secret" and "confidential." Attached to this is H. P. Swanton's memo of September 6, with the notation:

2. Attention is invited to paragraph 5 of first endorsement <Swanton's memo>.

Paragraph 5, of course, relates to the Master's trip to London and the subsequent one-day delay in sailing from Liverpool. Veasey thought it noteworthy enough to call to the attention of the Chief of Navy Operations. Unfortunately, because the context of the situation is unknown to us today, it is difficult to judge just what significance the delay had at the time the memo was written. Without doubt, having been written on September 9, it could not relate to the actual sinking of the *Esso Williamsburg.* Ironically, this memo is stamped as received by the Chief of Navy Operations on September 22, the day of the first attack on the *Esso Williamsburg*. Five more members of the Navy Armed Guard perished on the ill-fated *Esso Williamsburg*.

Baker, Glenn Harold

Maliszewski, Alexander Frank

Mathews, Glen David

McClintock, Thomas B.

Mealman, Roy Eric

Records received from the National Archives do not indicate when they were assigned to the ship, nevertheless, they are among the members of the Armed Guard presumed to have lost their lives on the ship, in spite of perplexing information later uncovered regarding their pay schedules.

One of them, Glenn Harold Baker, provides a fascinating and grim story that reflects the chaos associated with the assignment and tracking of the Navy Armed Guard personnel on merchant ships. On 19 December 1942, John J. Reynolds, by direction of Randall Jacobs, Chief of Navy Personnel, wrote to the Commanding Officer, Armed Guard Center in South Brooklyn, New York on the subject of BAKER, G. E., Signalman:

According to the information received in this Bureau the sub-ject-named man is reported as missing following the loss of the S. S. ESSO WILLIAMSBURG by enemy action during the month of September. This Bureau has no record, however, of any officer or enlisted man with such name and initials.

After requesting that information be forwarded "which will estab-lish his identity," the Chief of Navy Personnel goes on to request:

...that the Commanding Officer furnish this Bureau the last mus-ter roll of the Armed Guard Crew serving aboard the S. S. ESSO WILLIAMSBURG.

In a response, on December 23 William J. Coakley of the A.G.C. in Brooklyn wrote:

The subject man's (Baker, G.E.) records, accounts, and mail are not carried at this activity, and no information is available con-

cerning his being on board the S. S. ESSO WILLIAMSBURG at the time of the enemy action.

A muster list dated June 22, 1942 found in the records has a hand-written notation that the ship "Left Aruba on Sept. 11. Baker reported aboard at this time according to Master, Captain Tweed."

The next reference to the elusive Glenn Harold Baker occurs several years later, in the spring of 1944. A letter dated March 23 reflects a poignant story. The Armed Guard Center in New Orleans, Louisiana wrote to the Bureau of Navy Personnel regarding "BAKER, Glenn Harold" in reference to a letter received from his mother dated 17 January 1944:

Upon this command's receipt of reference (a) <above>, in which the mother of the subject named man inquired regarding her failure to hear from him since 6 June 1942, a communication was sent to the Commandant, 7th Navy District for information concerning his further assignment, as records of this Center indicate he was assigned to ComSEVEN for duty on 23 May 1942. Records and accounts were retained at this command, as subject man was on temporary detached duty. No information was received from ComSEVEN at that time regarding his assignment. In the absence of a reply, dispatches were sent on 7 February and 21 February 1944, in answer to which a reply was made by ComSEVEN that Baker was transferred to the SS ESSO WILLIAMSBURG 1 June 1942.

Payment records for Glenn Harold Baker are listed as 27 June 1942 by the Master of the *Esso Williamsburg* and shortly after <no date available> a payment of $48 by the Armed Guard Center in Brooklyn. Other payments include $10 at Cafac Curac, NWI, and $5.00 on August 24 and $24.21 on August 25 in Liverpool. Eerily enough, additional payments to Glenn Harold Baker indicate that the man was *not* on the *Williamsburg:*

There were two final undated payments made by the Armed Guard Center, Brooklyn, against this account, sometime during the quarter of October-December 1942. These payments, made by F. J. Scheel, were for $20.18 and $40.00.

The story of Glenn Baker continued. On May 24, 1944, A. C. Jacobs, Commander, Head of Casualties and Allotments Section, wrote to the

Commanding Officer at the A.G.C. in New Orleans regarding Glenn Harold Baker:

Upon investigation of the records of the United States Coast Guard it was found that a G. E. Baker, SM, was recorded as being on board the S. S. ESSO WILLIAMSBURG by Captain J. Tweed as of 23 August 1942. At the time of casualty to the S. S. ESSO WILLIAMSBURG, on or about 22 September 1942, it was not possible to find a G. E. BAKER in the records of this Bureau.

The complication that led to the "loss" of Glenn Harold Baker was a clerical one:

...it was found that subject named man's jacket <personnel file> contained a restricted communication...ordering...temporary duty as signalman aboard the S.S. ESSO WILLIAMSBURG. This restricted communication was, unfortunately, placed in the man's jacket when it should have gone to the Muster Roll Section.

Signalman Glenn Harold Baker was lost by the United States Navy and presumably was also lost at sea when the *Esso Williamsburg* was attacked and sunk. His story, however, continues. In a Navy memorandum dated 13 July 1944 the following event is recounted:

Subject named man <BAKER, Glenn Harold> is being carried as "missing" in the records of this Bureau. The mother of subject named man has a report that he is a Prisoner of War and the following is quoted from her letter of 3 June 1944:

"The Red Cross at Portland sent us word the first of April that the report had come in to them that Glenn Harold Baker was in a German Prison Camp and was well."

How could Glenn Baker have been in a German Prison Camp in April of 1944? Was this man truly on board the ship?

These unsolved mysteries reflect the chaos that surrounded the deployment of members of the Navy Armed Guard during World War II and of the war itself, chaos that added to the pain experienced by their next-of-kin.

THE U. S. NAVY ARMED GUARD

Almost 2,000 men of the U. S. Navy Armed Guard were reported killed or missing in World War II. They died valiantly, protecting the men and ships of the American merchant navy. They contributed greatly to the winning of World War II. We honor here the 18 members who died on the *Esso Williamsburg* <see Dedication Page>.

S2c James Greenwell, U. S. Navy
Armed Guard (LeRoy McClelland)

S2c Thomas B. McClintock, U. S. Navy Armed Guard
(Dick McClintock)

CHAPTER SIX

U-211

Keil, Germany 1941: The U-boat hub of the German Kriegsmarine. Here the boats are built, launched, and sent on shakedown cruises. In March of 1941 the keel for U-211 is laid in Keil, and the boat is launched on January 15 of 1942. She is a Type VII C boat, the most commonly used boat in the North Atlantic during the height of conflict. At her commissioning ceremony on March 7, 1942 a proud KL Karl Hause takes command.

Horst Bredow of the U-Boat Archives in Cuxhaven, Germany maintains the U-boat files. Courtesy of his archives, information and photographs provide insight into the men who sailed U-211. Kapitän-leutnantzur See (KL) Karl Hause is a slightly built man with narrow shoulders, a man of less than average height. In the commissioning photograph, his dark hair falls down across his forehead, slipping slightly below the brim of the jauntily placed officer's cap that perches on the right side of his head. He stands straight and proud in his obviously new blue uniform with its white belt and double row of brass buttons, a Navy sword hanging at his left side near his gloved hand. In the background, U-211 looms.

A second photo shows Hause standing with his officers, Karl-Heinz Schmidt, 1WO; Fritz Gross, Lt. Jg.; and Wolf Hellemeyer, 2WO. All but Hellemeyer wear the white belt; he was the youngest, and the best looking. These are clean-cut men with even features. The wind snaps across the deck of the submarine, whipping their coats astray. Other photos show the crew lined up for inspection, and the U-211 sailing out to sea, Swastika flying in the wind.

After the commissioning ceremony on March 7, U-211 is assigned to the 8th U-boat flotilla in Danzig, until August of 1942. On August 8, U-211 leaves for Arendal, Norway, arriving there on August 8. The boat sails from Arendal on the 18th and arrives in Bergen, Norway on the 24th. It should be noted that by this time Norway was thoroughly invaded by Germany and under the control of its military forces. Hence, the western coast of Norway was used by the Kriegsmarine not only as a destination for shakedown voyages but also as a launching point for U-boats assigned to patrols in the North Atlantic. U-211 was such a boat.

On August 16, KL Hause and the crew sail U-211 out of Bergen and on to operations in the North Atlantic. Her first assigned "wolf pack" is the Vorwärts group gathering west of Ireland. Vorwärts joins Stier group and forms a patrol line south of Iceland. On September 9, Convoy ON 127 is sighted by U-584 and the U-boats begin circling their prey, looking for the easiest pickings, the stragglers. During the next four days, they manage to sink seven ships and one corvette.

KL Hause and U-211, novices to war patrol, did well. On September 12, they shoot two torpedoes and damage *Hektoria* (12,797 tons), a large British ship, and a smaller ship, the *SS Empire Moonbeam* (6,849 tons). The coups de grᐧs, however, are delivered by the more experienced U-608. Still, this was not bad shooting for a green commander and his crew.

Hektoria, in particular, is a hugh hit for U-211, even though she didn't sink the ship. The former White Star Line passenger ship *SS Medic* built in 1899, this ship had capacity for 320 cabin class passengers. She was in Boer War service and in 1928 was refitted as a whaling ship. *Hektoria* is now carrying oil for the British Ministry of War.

Out of a crew of 86, only one loses his life in the ship's sinking. In terms of tonnage sunk, *Hektoria*, at almost 12,000 tons, is a prize.

Even though U-608 is credited with the kill, it still looks good for U-211 to have accomplished the initial attack on *Hektoria* on its first patrol. As the former *SS Medic*, the ship was beautiful, a jewel of the White Star Line.

Next, KL Hause spots the *SS Empire Moonbeam*, the Rear Commodore ship for Convoy ON-127, through his periscope. He shoots a torpedo and damages the 6,849 ton merchant ship. The next day, September 13, U-608 delivers the coup de grᐧs and sinks *Empire Moonbeam*. The Canadian corvette *HMCS Arvida* rescues the ship's master, 44 crew, six gunners and one passenger. Three crew members are lost. *HMCS Arvida* also rescues the *Hektoria* survivors.

Arvida brings the rescued men to St. John, Newfoundland, a city where thousands of rescued merchant sailors find refuge during the worst days of the Battle of the Atlantic.

Meanwhile, back in the North Atlantic, U-211 begins to have mechanical problems. The boat refuels at one of the "milk cows" in the area and crew members work on a slipping gear. After refueling, she leaves to catch up with the Vorwärts group.

And then, in one of those fatal coincidences that so frequently occur in war, U-211 accidentally encounters the *Esso Williamsburg* as that ship was speeding for Iceland with her cargo of Navy fuel. U-211, however, was supposed to be joining Vorwärts group to attack the next convoy coming through this most dangerous stretch of the North Atlantic. As a result, before attacking, she radios Kriegsmarine Headquarters for permission to pursue and attack the *Esso Williamsburg*.

In terms of displacement, U-211 weighs a little over 1,000 tons, considerably smaller than the *Esso Williamsburg*, which weighs in at over 11,000 tons. Surface speed is comparable. The *Williamsburg* is said to have a top speed of 17 knots, while U-211, a Type VIII C, is rated at 17 knots on the surface, but only 7.6 knots below the surface. U-211 could keep up with the *Williamsburg* on the surface but then ran the danger of being spotted by planes or other surface convoy escort ships. When submerged, U-211 is considerably slower than the tanker.

After sinking the *Esso Williamsburg* <see Chapter 3, Search>, U-211 joins Vorwärts again in pursuit of convoy RB 1, comprised of steamers from the Great Lakes enroute to England. In the evening hours of the 24th and 25th, U-211 unsuccessfully attacks a ship in this convoy. After this, she leaves the area and heads to her new "home," the 9th U-boat flotilla in Brest, France. She heads home elated, having had a very successful voyage for a new boat. She arrives Brest on October 7.

After a little more than five weeks rest, U-211 again sets out for the North Atlantic on November 16. In December, a group forms west of Ireland to track convoy ON 153.

Early on December 17th, U-211 torpedoes *HMS Firedrake*. U-211's attack on the *Firedrake* receives no more attention in the history books than the other sinkings in the area at the time. The story of the *Firedrake* and its rescue ship, HMS *Sunflower*, however, graphically portrays the havoc wrought by U-boats in general and U-211 in particular. Convoy ON 153, 43 ships bound for Canada on the night of December 16, had *HMS Firedrake*, an F class destroyer, as its lead escort. A force 12 storm is battering the ships.

One survivor of *Firedrake*, Donald J. L. Coombes, describes the weather at the time of the attack as so bad that even before the destroyer was cut in half by U-211's torpedo, crew members were in danger of being swept overboard. In danger of being washed overboard, they would phone when leaving the stern of the destroyer and phone again on arrival at the bow.

According to Coombes, it looks like U-211 is again meeting her prey by happenstance. He recalls that the sub had surfaced, apparently for battery charging and ventilation, and was surprised to see *Firedrake* close by. Weather is interfering with Asdic and radar detection systems on *Firedrake.*

In the midst of the storm, U-211 attacks with one torpedo. *Firedrake's* bow sinks. The radio and signaling equipment in the bow are now gone. The stern stays afloat.

According to Lt. D. J. Dampier, RN who is on the stern, 60 foot waves prevailed. Here's his description of the corvette HMS *Sunflower's* attempts at rescuing the crew of *Firedrake*:

> When "Sunflower" came as near alongside as she could get, it was decided to take survivors off by boson's chair, but with the corvette at one point towering some sixty feet above us and the next sixty feet below in that mighty sea no such action was possible. It was decided therefore to wait for daybreak before transferring to the rescue ship.

Peter Collins, Ordinary Signalman on HMS *Sunflower*, remembers a particularly heroic shipmate of his, George Furey, a Newfoundlander, who manages to rescue *Firedrake* survivors in a most unique and dangerous fashion. Furey:

> ...tied a life line around his waist and gone overboard into the icy sea, could see where the men were, so he could grab hold of them, when he had hold of one he would be pulled back to the ship where the survivor would be helped aboard. George managed to save twenty-seven of the Firedrake's crew this way but one died before daylight. These twenty-six were the only sur-

vivors from the Firedrake on that terrible night. I still see in my mind's eye that horrific scene of young men putting their arms up, and slipping out of their life-belts so they would go under quicker because they knew that they were too far from the Sunflower to be rescued.

John Dixon, another *Sunflower* crew member, has another vivid memory of the rescue:

In the beam of light a rubber dinghy was momentary illuminated, with two men inboard. One of the men was stretched out, not moving, the other man had a small paddle which he was using in his attempt to make his way towards our ship's side. The moment the light flashed on him I saw and heard him call out for us to help those men who were still in the water before rescuing them both. The two men were probably duty stokers from the engine room, as they only had vests and trouser overalls on. The hands of the man who was paddling were blackened and appeared to have been badly burnt, but he seamed to be void of experiencing pain.

Of a crew of 194, only six officers and 20 ratings are rescued. U-211 has killed another 168 men.

During its first patrols in the autumn of 1942, U-211 was responsible for the death of 232 men and assisted in or sank three merchant ships and one British corvette. U-211 returned to Brest on December 29.

On Feb. 13, 1943 she left for operations again in the North Atlantic. On February 20, she was depth-charged and damaged in the Bay of Biscay by a U. S. Air Force Liberator and returned again to Brest on the 25th. Here she remained until May 10, l943. After unsuccessful attempts to locate convoys, U-211 returned to Lorient on July 16. Here she remained until September 23, when she sailed for Brest, arriving on the 24th.

On November 16, 1943 U-211 embarks on her last patrol. Assigned by Kriegsmarine headquarters to meet up with seven other U-boats, she joins "Schill 1," a wolf pack assigned to track convoys east of the Azore Islands. Schill is ordered to remain submerged in daylight, to surface at 6:30 p.m., and to switch to D/F reception. Two reconnaissance flights are scheduled to patrol the area in the daylight hours, providing an umbrella of protection for the U-boats. These planes

sight a convoy of 64 ships, three destroyers and four corvettes. Schill is ordered to begin attacking the convoy on the evening of the 18th. U-515 sends out this message:

While making <transmitting> radio message at 1500 forced to dive by an A/S group. 2 T5 misses. Heavy D/C's. Am carrying out repairs.

Anti-submarine forces had caused the sub to dive quickly. Two depth charges narrowly missed U-515.

Group Schill races around the area in which the convoy is progressing. Dönitz receives another message, as recorded in his diary:

Another obscure message <u>without signature</u> was received at 0200 (Nov. 18). It read: "Convoy CF 5348, 12 o'clock, speed 12 knots, <u>am unable to dive</u>".

The unknown sub was probably the U-211. Dönitz's report at first indicates that the unknown sub was probably U-333:

The boat which reported herself unable to dive during the night 18/19 was probably U 333.

Two points are important here. Now the diary reads that the message was received during the night of 18/19, not at 2 a.m. on November 18. The second point is that U-333 is reported to have been sunk on July 31, 1944 by two British sloops and a frigate, somewhere west of the Scilly Islands. All other boats in the Schill group were accounted for.

It was not until December 6 that Dönitz referred to the possible loss of U-211:

U 211 was operating within Group "Schill 1" (CF 53) on the north-bound convoy and was ordered to return on 20 November in view of fuel shortage. This boat also has not yet sent in her arrival report, which is due. She must, therefore, be considered lost. Loss almost certainly occurred off the convoy. Cause unknown, but probably by aircraft.

As became known at the war's end, U-211 was attacked and sunk east of the Azores on November 19 by depth charges dropped from a British Wellington airplane of Squadron 179/F. It appears safe to assume that it was indeed U-211 that reported it was unable to dive and therefore became a prime target for the anti-submarine forces operating in the area. In any event, U-211 was never heard from again.

U-211's last patrol appears to have been a deadly one by virtue of not only the increasing superiority of anti-submarine forces operating in the area but also because of some modifications made to the boat prior to the last patrol. U-211 was one of a few boats that had been converted to "Flak U-boats."

Immediately after reporting that U-211 was probably destroyed, Dönitz goes on to state in his report that the design was being scrapped and all existing Flak U-boats were being converted back to their original Type VII C design. The enlarged bridge structure necessary for mounting anti-aircraft guns made the boats top-heavy, a particular problem in heavy seas. Hydrodynamically, these boats created more resistance and that increased diving time and reduced underwater speed. Adding additional guns meant that more men would be on the sub's deck. Thus, it took more time to clear the deck, before submerging. Fuel capacity was reduced. The Flak subs could carry only five torpedoes. Dönitz reported that allied planes would circle just out of the firing range of the Flak subs and wait until surface ships and other aircraft arrived, before diving in for the kill. Trying to make U-boats into surface fighting ships just didn't work.

One wonders if the men of U-211 fully understood the weaknesses of their boat's modifications, before leaving on their last patrol. U-211 was most definitely a boat fingered for death by an ill-conceived attempt on the part of the Kriegsmarine command to turn the tide of World War II in their favor.

In the same way as the *Esso Williamsburg* had limped away from U-211 after her first attack, U-211 tried to evade anti-submarine forces while unable to dive. Neither made it.

RAF Squadron 179 got the credit for sinking U-211 on November 19, 1943. As the record states, "54 Gefallene." Wolf Hellemeyer (age 23) and Fritz Gross (age 25) went down with Hause. Karl-Heinz Schmidt transferred off before the boat was sunk. The oldest man on board was 34-year-old Omasch Willi Mühl. The youngest was

MaschGfr Werner Fellmuth, 19-years-old. Five other 19-year-olds were on that boat. Hause himself was 27 when he died.

Also in the U-boat Archives file is a copy of U-211's emblem. Ironically, considering my father's nationality, it was a Viking ship.

Captain and officers of U-211. (U-boot-Archiv, Cuxhaven, Germany)

The U-211 going out to sea. (U-boot-Archiv, Cuxhaven, Germany)

MS Firedrake. (United gdom Government, Public Domain)

CHAPTER SEVEN

LIFEBOAT

Captain Arthur Moore has considerable knowledge on the fate of merchant ships and their crews. He dedicates his book, <u>A Careless Word, A Needless Sinking</u>, "To the Officers and Men who sailed the ships of the U. S. Merchant Marine during World War II, and especially to those who lost their lives, and to their families." His book is a comprehensive collection of artifacts and information related to the merchant marine in World War II. In the preface, Captain Moore acknowledges what he was *not* able to do in his book:

> *As this is a reference book, it does not tell of the sufferings of the men struggling to survive in crowded lifeboats or on flimsy rafts. Nor does it tell of the dust-dry throats, the parched lips and swollen tongues of those with no fresh water. Nor does it tell of the agony they suffered from being cramped in a crowded lifeboat for days on end, unable to stretch their legs. Neither does it describe the frozen limbs of those adrift in boats on the North Atlantic or the Barents Sea and the horror in the engine rooms where men faced scalding steam from exploding boilers and ruptured steam lines....How could a reference book describe the emotions of the survivors of the torpedoed Harry Luckenbach as they sat in their lifeboats watching three escort vessels pass them by in plain sight...none survived.*

Robert Browning's book, <u>U. S. Merchant Vessel War Casualties of World War II</u>, refers to a weak distress signal being sent from the *Esso Williamsburg* as it was being attacked. Captain Moore's narrative of the missing *Esso Williamsburg's* last voyage gives even more chilling information:

> On September 24 <after the sinking>, a weak distress signal was received from one of the ESSO WILLIAMSBURG's lifeboats giving a position of 53-10 North/41.00 West.

Perhaps a few crewmembers had escaped that burning inferno on September 23. Comparing the position of the lifeboat to that of the reported attack (53-12 North/41.00 West) reveals that the lifeboat sailed 2 degrees to the southwest while sending the distress signal.

In January of 1999, I contacted Captain Arthur Moore and on April 14, he replies:

> Thank you for your letter re: "Esso Williamsburg." It is so sad when a ship just disappears and we know nothing of what happened. There were 32 other U. S. flag vessels that disappeared the same way. I have all the logs of the subs that sank these ships and it makes me so crazy that the sub C.O. didn't stick around at least long enough to find out about survivors.

> I don't know what edition you've seen of my book but in the latest one (1998) I have a complete translation of the log of U-211 in Addendum II. I note in it that the sub C.O. never said a word about survivors except he saw an empty life raft. But then I fault the U. S. Navy for sending these ships out alone. I don't care if they were fast, they still got hit and no escort around to pick up survivors. This country was so unprepared for WWII. The more I research the sicker I get.

> Unfortunately I lost the source of my statement in the book about the message from the lifeboat. But if you note the location of the sinking you'll see it's not far from the position of the lifeboat.

He goes on to refer specifically to the doomed *Esso Williamsburg* and the revelation that the crew had indeed managed to launch lifeboats!

I got a letter from a Captain Renhave, an ex Esso skipper from 1941-1983. He heard from "old-timers" that Capt. Tweed got one or 2 boats in the water probably before the final torpedo. He got off a message saying, "We are heading into the Sun." He (Capt. Renhave) said that was heard by several ships.

Capt. Moore's letter continues:

The govt. never made any effort to research the loss of these ships that disappeared with all hands...I found all my data in a German book and my book was the first to reveal the story. I've had many families write to thank me for finding out what happened to their loved ones and that makes me feel good!

"We are heading into the Sun." What did this mean? That the lifeboats were heading that way, or that the *Esso Williamsburg* was sailing in that direction? Was it morning or afternoon? And why did none of the "several ships" that heard Captain Tweed's poignant message respond?

Herein lies a harsh reality of this war at sea. Bernard Edwards, author of <u>Dönitz and the Wolf Packs, The U-Boats at War</u>, quotes the captain of the *Manchester Merchant*, a ship that had just been torpedoed:

I looked over the fore part of the bridge and saw water pouring over the forecastle head. The ship was settling rapidly by the head, and as she was obviously doomed I ordered 'abandon ship, every man for himself'...but before I could abandon ship...I was washed off the bridge deck into the sea by the force of water rushing over the ship. I was pulled under by the suction...I could hear men screaming and shouting all around me, and saw lots of small lifebelt lights bobbing about on the swell... After about half an hour, the destroyer...came along and rescued fifteen men who were on a raft, but went away leaving the remainder of the survivors in the water. I suppose she had some reason for going away, but when the men in the water saw the destroyer going, their cries were terrible, and from the splashing in the water I imagine they must have tried to follow...I could only hear moans for a while, and then silence.

Whether from a fear of dying themselves, a blind obedience to orders, or a sense that their ships and cargoes were too precious to the war effort to be further put in harm's way, few vessels stopped to assist survivors in lifeboats. Recognition must be given, however, to the rescue vessels of the U. S. Coast Guard, the Canadian Navy, and the British Navy that regularly ran the gamut of "Torpedo Junction" in search of survivors. In particular, the U. S. Coast Guard cutters *Bibb* and *Ingham* served very well in the very worst of times and circumstances.

Next, a new source is found in the United Kingdom via the Internet:

The U-boat Association is an association for victims of U-boats during World War II. Membership is open to surviving victims and to next-of-kin. Others interested in the U-boat campaign and the role of the merchant seamen can join as associate members. Membership is free, but donations from members are welcomed to keep the association going. A regular newsletter is produced, which features appeals for help and information and accounts of various aspects of the Battle of the Atlantic. You can get more details by writing to:

U-boat Association,

6, Wilton Drive,

Whitley Bay,NE25 9PU

United Kingdom

Soon I am a member of the U-Boat Association and begin receiving their quarterly newsletter in which they post my inquiry regarding the sinking of the *Esso Williamsburg* by U-211. Then, in one of those unlikely coincidences that characterize the randomness of research and pure providence of results comes news so startling that it is almost doubtful.

On April 4, 2000 a letter arrives from a Harry Hutson in Cleethorpes, Lincolnshire, United Kingdom:

I saw your request in the current issue of "The U-Boat Association" newsletter. Here is what I have on ESSO WILLIAMSBURG.

His letter goes on to state that:

...a weak SOS was received from one lifeboat and air/sea searches were organized and a destroyer (nationality not given) made radio contact with the lifeboat (I have the details of exchanges made by radio)....

Harry Hutson's amazing revelation is the first substantial lead that reinforces Captain Arthur Moore's report:

On September 24 <the day after the sinking>, a weak distress signal was received from one of the ESSO WILLIAMSBURG's lifeboats giving a position of 53-10 North/41.00 West.

I receive additional information from Harry in the end of April, 2000:

I enclose a photo-copy of the transmissions between the lifeboat and the destroyer. Unfortunately I do not have the source of my information because in the early days of my interest in research of the war at sea, I did not fully appreciate the consequences of such unforgiveable neglect. I have been doing this for over 30 years now and have amassed a hugh private collection of information (and over 1,000 books) on the subject.

He goes on to state:

You may not be aware that ESSO WILLIAMSBURG must have been fitted with the very latest lifeboat transmitter/receiver of American design and manufacture...The American lifeboat set... was designed to be held between the thighs, and fitted with a cranked generator. You will see a reference to the men becoming very tired due to cranking—it was quite a task to keep it up for a lengthy period of time—the transmitter was made of heavy metal and was painted bright yellow. A supply of rocket launched kites to carry the antenna was also supplied.

Radio transmissions were recorded using Greenwich Mean Time. To make the chronology of events more understandable, hours here are expressed in Standard Time. The ship was sunk in the early morning hours of September 23 (or around midnight of the 22nd, depending on the time system being used). Therefore, the men could have been in the lifeboat as long as two days before a destroyer operating in the vicinity picked up their desperate transmission:

Sept. 25 (two days after the sinking of the *Esso Williamsburg*):

5:54 p.m. 53.10N 41.02W

From COAC – General. Distress signal from lifeboat.

7:00 p.m.

From destroyer to SO escort. Am steering course to pass through reported position of lifeboat, reference COAC 1854 <see above>

10:22 p.m.

From destroyer to COAC – Immediate – Ask lifeboat WTKJ to transmit on 500Kc/s as I am in vicinity.

Since the coordinates of the *Esso Williamsburg*'s sinking were 53:12N 41:00W, the lifeboat at 53:10N 41:02W was about one-and-a-half statute miles southwest of that area, when its first transmission was picked up. <Or, perhaps estimates of the sinking location were based on transmissions from the lifeboat. We simply don't know.> About nine hours elapsed, before the next transmission on the following day:

Sept. 26

7:45 a.m.

From destroyer to lifeboat – Keep transmitting, we are trying to take a bearing.

7:50 a.m. 53.30N 41.00W

From lifeboat – SOS We were carrying Navy fuel to Iceland when struck. Approx. position 53.30N 41.00W SOS.

From 53:10N 41:02W the previous night to the coordinates given on September 26 of 53:30N 41:00W by the men in the lifeboat, it appears they sailed almost 14 statute miles to the northeast in nine hours.
September 26 continues:

7:58 a.m.

From Lifeboat – In Gods name send help quickly. We were swamped yesterday and could not send other messages. SOS SOS

8:10 a.m.

From destroyer – Received your signals. Make Z and long dashes if you can hear us.

8:38 a.m. 53.30N 41.00W

SOS from WTKJ – Our approx position 53.30N 41W we will send 30 minutes after each hour so you can get a D/F bearing on us. Please hurry and get us in Gods name.

10:59 a.m.

From destroyer – Can you hear me please, go ahead now. If you can hear me call me with call sign Abner.

Another hour transpires before the destroyer, code sign Abner, hears another transmission from the lifeboat. Apparently the men in the lifeboat did not hear Abner's request of 10:59 a.m.

12:00 noon

SOS Lifeboat WTKJ Williamsburg. Badly in need of water and medical assistance.

Two hours later, the destroyer responds:

1:55 p.m.

From destroyer – We are coming to your aid. Keep sending. Our call sign is Abner. Can you hear me now?

2:00 p.m.

From lifeboat to Abner – Yes and thanks to God old man to you we will send from here on the hour and 30 minutes after the hour as the men get very tired from cranking the generator.

2:25 p.m.

From Abner – I am going to drop a depth charge in five minutes. Let me know if you hear it.

2:35 p.m.

From Lifeboat – We did not hear your depth charge.

3:45 p.m.

From Lifeboat – Will send again in 10 minutes.

Not ten but 32 minutes later, the lifeboat manages another transmission:

4:17 p.m.

SOS from lifeboat WTKJ – Need medical aid and water immediately will send again in fifteen minutes.

4:33 p.m.

From WTKJ lifeboat - The sun has just broken through to the west of us. We have a bright orange flag up from a 20 ft. mast we did not hear your gun fired or depth charge.

5:18 p.m.

The sun is shining and the sea is very slightly choppy. We have to use oars to keep from being swamped. The wind is blowing us outter <sic> to sea.

And then what must have appeared to be salvation:

5:30 p.m.

From lifeboat - We just sighted you NE of us and coming closer. We are firing a flare in a few minutes.

Fate once again, however, intervenes:

5:35 p.m.

From lifeboat — Flare pistol won't work but you appear to be steering towards us.

5:40 p.m.

From lifeboat — The ship that we sighted was 2 to 5 miles away. Is that you?

Abner takes the initiative:

5:42 p.m.

From Abner — Am going to fire a rocket. Report if you can see it.

6:00 p.m.

From lifeboat — We are between you and the sun.

6:10 p.m.

From lifeboat — The ship we see has one stack.

One stack, however, is not consistent with a destroyer.

6:15 p.m.

From Abner – Did you see my rocket? Or hear my charge?

6:28 p.m.

From Abner – Am I still steering for you?

The last entry reads:

The lifeboat was never found, only wreckage.

For those last 40 minutes, from 5:30 p.m. on September 26 until shortly after 6:10 p.m., these men thought they were saved. What cruel irony to die, when help was so close by. The sun had just come out and shone upon them.

They saw the rescue vessel approaching. And then fate intervened once again, this time for the final time. One logical assumption is that a rogue wave in that "slightly choppy sea" dashed their tiny boat to pieces. Or, perhaps a U-boat lurking in the vicinity and waiting for the destroyer, destroyed the small lifeboat.

How many men were in the lifeboat? How had they left the ship in those final few minutes? Was a lifeboat lowered on the port side in the few minutes before the coup de grâs was delivered to starboard? This, at least, could account for the U-211's report of seeing no survivors.

Possibly the lifeboats were swung out soon after the first attack, as the ship was limping away. Probably the boats were checked for equipment, in particular, for the radio, flares, and signal flags reported by the men in the lifeboat.

Plausible, then, is the assumption that water and medical supplies were available. The report of being swamped indicates that supplies might have been lost overboard. That water and medical aid were critical to these men is clear from their plaintive cries.

CHAPTER EIGHT

SEARCH FOR THE DESTROYER

Much time has been spent in trying to locate the name of the destroyer that sought so valiantly to rescue the men in the *Esso Williamsburg's* lifeboat. If that destroyer's Deck Log could be located, surely more clues would be found as to its demise.

Finding the destroyer proved to be as difficult as locating a drifting lifeboat. But the search gives an impressive snapshot of exactly what was going on in the North Atlantic in September of 1942. It was chaos.

Finding one lifeboat in the North Atlantic, even with location coordinates and radio communications, was an almost hopeless task in September of 1942. Even in peacetime, it is difficult to find a sailboat in distress in blue water.

Modern-day GPS technology and EPERB signal devices both aid rescue ships and planes in locating their targets today. Neither, however, was available in 1942.

To envision the Battle of the Atlantic in September of 1942, picture a clock. At 12 o'clock in this mental framework is Greenland, with the tip of Cape Farewell jutting down toward center. At two o'clock is Iceland, the center for aircraft and rescue ships in that area. At 3 to 4 o'clock is the United Kingdom, the coastlines of Scotland and Ireland forming the right side of the clock. At 6 o'clock is the bottom of the clock, the South Atlantic with the Azores slightly to the east. At 9 o'clock, the rugged coast of Canada: Nova Scotia with Halifax as the convoy shipping center, and Newfoundland, another center for convoy escort ships.

Right in the center of this mental clock is an area known as the Greenland Air Gap, the Black Hole, Torpedo Junction, and MOMP <Mid-Ocean Meeting Point>. Very Long Range (VLR) aircraft were in short supply. Planes leaving from the Canadian coast, Iceland, or the United Kingdom simply could not carry enough fuel to reach this center area to provide convoy air cover. Hence, it became the prime attack ground for U-boat packs patrolling the North Atlantic.

West-East convoys, those going from Canada to the U.K., began their voyages surrounded by convoy escort groups: Canadian, British and American destroyers, corvettes, minesweepers and cutters. These escorts would take them to MOMP, where a convoy escort group from Iceland would be waiting to pick up the ships, sometimes as many as 100, and escort them to the far side. Sooner or later, that escort group in turn would hand the convoy over to a convoy escort group coming out from the U.K., and that escort would bring whatever ships remained afloat into various ports in the U.K. East-West convoys followed the reverse procedure.

Just the very task of finding convoys in the North Atlantic was hugh. Incessant attacks from U-boat wolf packs were made. Once spotting a convoy, U-boats would race up and down the lanes between the ships, picking off the easy prey first, then hunkering down for battles with the more formidable escort ships. Add on the harrowing weather of the North Atlantic, the interminable gales where 35 foot waves were commonplace and hurricane force winds sliced across the decks of the ships, hurling sailors to the wind.

For those mariners and sailors who survived U-boat attacks and were able to get into lifeboats, the initial reaction was relief at having escaped the explosions, fires, and drowning. All too soon, however, the reality of their plight became apparent. Ships sailed by and would not stop to pick them up, fearing that lurking U-boats in the area waited to pounce on rescue ships. When no ships were visible, lifeboats desperately attempted to send out messages on the radio-telephones or, if not so equipped, settled for shooting flares into the air, hoping escort ships might sight their signal. Even worse, they were tossed about in the seas, minuscule chips, freezing, soaked with salt water, thirsty and starving. Chances of being rescued diminished as time marched on. Death was almost certain, a lingering painful death.

At the time the *Esso Williamsburg* was torpedoed and sunk, in the days immediately after, when its sole lifeboat was adrift sending out desperate messages for help, four important convoys were in play: RB-1, ON-131, and SC-100 and SC-101.

Convoy RB-1

Convoy RB-1 left St. Johns, Newfoundland on 21 September comprised of eight merchant ships sailing in four columns. Escort ships were the destroyers *HMS Vanoc* (Senior Officer) and *HMS Veteran.*, each 25 years old and two of the oldest ships in Her Majesty's Navy. Eight merchant ships included *SS Boston* (commodore), *SS New York*, *SS Yorktown*, *SS New Bedford*, *SS Naushon*, *SS Northland*, *SS Southland* and *SS President Warfield*.

RB-1 had an interesting code name: Maniac. Indeed, in retrospect it does seem maniacal to believe that such a group had even a chance of making the Atlantic crossing intact. RB stood for "river boats." The ships were coastal and river vessels and not sea-going vessels. The crews were volunteers. In some instances, not enough food was onboard to sustain the crews as their ships inched across the Atlantic. Reports showed that plywood facades had been installed on some of the ships to give them the appearance of troop transport carriers.

Moreover, there were post-war reports that Admiral Dönitz had been convinced that RB-1 was a troop-carrying convoy. As a result, he sent wolf packs Vorwarts (10 U-boats) and Pfiel (7 U-boats) to intercept the ill-fated convoy. U-211, assigned to Vorwarts, was racing to join that group, after refueling to the south. It was during this dash that U-211 encountered the *Esso Williamsburg* and radioed for permission to pursue and sink her. Permission was needed, because U-211 would be deviating from orders in pursuit of the lone tanker. So it was by happenstance of "decoy" convoy RB-1 that U-211 and *Esso Williamsburg* met in that vast North Atlantic furor.

Of the ships in Convoy RB-1, *SS Boston*, *SS New York*, and *SS Yorktown* were sunk by the enemy. Moreover, *HMS Veteran*, after picking up survivors from these attacks, was sunk on 26 September in the early morning hours. We know that it was not *Veteran* who answered the call of the *Esso Williamsburg's* lifeboat, because the lifeboat was still in contact with the nameless destroyer coming to rescue them until the late afternoon hours of 26 September. By that time, *Veteran* had been sunk. If indeed RB-1 was a decoy, the question follows as to what circumstances called for a decoy. Convoy ON-131 may well be the answer.

Convoy ON-131

ON-131 sailed from the United Kingdom on 18 September, leaving Cardiff bound for Halifax, and was due to arrive on 28 September. While wolf packs Vorwarts and Pfiel were racing toward Canada to attack RB-1's pathetic little group of eight ships, ON-131 with 62 ships in ballast sailed with apparent ease, protected by a Canadian escort group comprised of the destroyers *HMCS Saguenay* and *HMCS Skeena*.

Of the 62 ships in this convoy, only one, the *SS John Winthrop* (American) straggled behind the convoy and was sunk by U-619. There were no survivors from the *John Winthrop*. Eventually, ON-131 arrived in New York on October 4.

The safe arrival of 61 ships from ON-131 certainly compensated for the loss of three merchant vessels and one British destroyer from RB-1. If indeed RB-1, code name Maniac, was intended as a decoy, it surely worked.

Convoy SC-100

The third convoy in the area was SC-100, sailing from Halifax on 12 September with an estimated arrival date of 28 September in Liverpool. American Escort Group A3 under the command of Captain Paul R. Heineman, USN was assigned. Heinemann chose the U. S. Coast Guard cutter *Spencer* as his flag ship, making *Spencer* the Senior Officer ship. USCG cutters *Campbell, Bibb* and *Ingham* were also attached to this group of 20 ships bound for the U.K.

Canadian corvettes *Weyburn, Lunenburg, Bittersweet, Mayflower, Rosthern, Trillium* and *Dauphin* were also attached, as well as the British corvette *Nasturtium*. Comparing this large escort group to RB-1 with eight ships and two old destroyers as escort tends to confirm the decoy story. However, even with such a large escort group, SC-100 lost four ships during the crossing.

The first to go was the *SS Athelsultan* on 23 September, followed closely by *SS Penmar*, a straggler, on 24 September. Two men were lost; 60 survived. USCG cutters *Bibb* and *Ingham* became involved, when they sailed to a position about 700 miles southwest of Iceland with a small group of ten ships.

They were to exchange these ten ships for the twenty ships in SC-100. American Escort Group A3 under Paul Heinemann then brought the ten ships from Iceland back to Halifax. *Bibb* and *Ingham* next joined the remainder of SC-100. They performed well. *Bibb* went off to search for survivors of *Penmar*, after seeing a red flare. After a three hour search following a trail of debris, she found a lifeboat and a raft from *Penmar*. She rescued 61 survivors from *Penmar*. Meanwhile, *Ingham* raced about searching for and finally rescuing eight survivors of the *SS Tennessee*, which had been sunk on 23 September. Ten survivors of *SS Athelsultan* were picked up by *HMCS Weyburn* and *HMS Nasturtium* and ultimately landed at Londonderry.

Ship logs from *Spencer*, *Campbell*, *Ingham* and *Bibb* make no mention of radio contact with a lifeboat from the *Esso Williamsburg*. All of the above sinkings occurred in grids AK or AL to the north or east of the *Esso Williamsburg's* demise. Escort ships were dashing back and forth in the area of the *Williamsburg's* lifeboat. Some lifeboats got lucky and were located and rescued. The *Williamsburg's* lifeboat was, unfortunately, not one of these.

Of the escort ships in the area, only the destroyers *HMCS Saguenay* and *HMCS Skeena* seem to be possible potential rescuers of the *Esso Williamsburg's* lifeboat. A close look at their photos, however, reveals one factor that would deny their involvement. Both have two smokestacks. The men in the lifeboat radioed, "The ship we see has one stack."

Convoy SC 101

Also in the North Atlantic area at the time of the *Esso Williamsburg's* sinking was Convoy SC 101, en route from Halifax, N.S. to Liverpool, England. It departed on September 19 with approximately 16 merchant ships of British, Dutch, Norwegian, Danish, Icelandic, Greek, American, and Panamian ownership. Also in the group was a Ministry of War Transport, the *Tovalil*. Of these ships, only the British ship *Lifland* did not survive. She was torpedoed and sunk by U-610 on 29 September.

However, the important information on SC 101 is its escort ships, which were plentiful. Among the destroyers was *HMCS Annapolis*, an old destroyer with four stacks. *HMCS Restigouche*, a River Class destroyer, *HMCS St. Croix*, a Town Class destroyer. The destroyers had at least two stacks. A U. S. Navy destroyer, the USS Leary, sailed with them.

Also escorting SC 101 was the armed yacht *HMCS Elk*, two minesweepers *HMCS Grandmere* and *HMCS Lachine*. *HMCS Thunder*, either a destroyer or a minesweeper, joined the group. Moreover, U.

S. Coast Guard cutters included *USCGC Bibb* and *USCGC Ingham*, both of which joined the convoy while en route, and the *USS Leary*.

Of more than passing interest is the array of corvettes escorting Convoy SC 101. These escorts included *HMCS Amherst*, a Flower Class corvette; *HMCS Arvida*; *HMCS Celandine*; *HMCS Kamsack*; *HMCS Sherbrooke*; and *HMCS Sorel*. Corvettes are of interest to this story. World War II corvettes had one stack. Could it be that the men in the *Esso Williamsburg's* lifeboat spotted a corvette, not the actual destroyer with whom they were in contact?

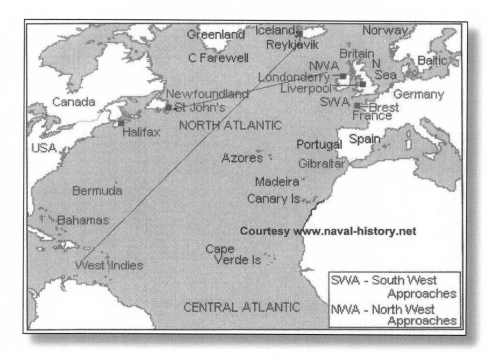

Courtesy www.naval-history.net

SWA - South West Approaches
NWA - North West Approaches

On August 24, 1942 U-211 sailed from Norway to Kiel, Germany. Two days later she sailed for the North Atlantic and joined wolf pack Vorwarts, operating east of Newfoundland. On September 12 *Esso Williamburg* sailed from Aruba (West Indies) for Reykjavik, Iceland with a cargo of Navy fuel. On September 22, about 500 miles south of Cape Farewell, Greenland U-211 torpedoed and sank *Esso Williamsburg*. At the time, U-211 was operating alone, and *Esso Williamsburg* was sailing independently and without convoy protection. (Map: www. naval-history.net)

CHAPTER NINE

MYSTERY SOLVED

Like a really good mystery story, the saga of the *Esso Williamsburg's* lifeboat is finally solved insofar as identifying the mysterious destroyer that gallantly rushed to the assistance of those crew members who died so tragically close to rescue. In the early autumn of 2010, the writer received a private message, posted on the forum of uboat.net, sent by someone named "Warwick." Warwick turns out to be pivotal in solving the mystery of the destroyer.

Warwick Lister's uncle, Harold Cedric Linton, had been an engineer on the *Esso Williamsburg*. His family, too, had been wondering over the years about the final demise of the ship and its men. They had many questions. Warwick and his brother, however, made the discovery that *HMCS Skeena*, a Canadian destroyer, was the ship in contact with the lifeboat more than fifty years earlier.

Even more intriguing, the story had been told in a publication of the Royal Canadian Navy in 1957.

1957, the U. S. Government had *not* contacted any family members with additional information regarding the ship and its crew, so it must be assumed that the government was unaware of a story published in <u>Crowsnest</u>, a journal of the Royal Canadian Navy. In February of 1957, Hal Lawrence wrote an article for the publication entitled "Am I Still Steering for You?" Lawrence, a retired officer of the Royal Canadian Navy, discovered in the signal log of *HMCS Skeena* a sad and intriguing account of the destroyer's attempts to rescue merchant sailors foundering in a lifeboat in September of 1942. Lawrence became well-known as the author of <u>Victory At Sea</u>.

While the article cannot be reprinted here verbatim, the essence of the story is that *Skeena* was part of Convoy ON 131 <61 merchant ships> en route from the U.K., departing Liverpool on September 18 to WOMP <Western Ocean Meeting Place>, along with *Saguenay* and 15 other escort vessels. Both destroyers had just depth charged a submarine attempting to sink ships in their convoy. The sub got away.

After that, *Skeena* discovered a problem with sea water in her fuel tanks. It was serious enough so that *Saguenay*, the senior escort vessel, ordered *Skeena* to return to St. John's, Newfoundland for repairs.

Skeena left the convoy and set her compass for St. John's. A quick dash for that harbor would bring them to relative safety.

At this point, COAC <Commanding Office Atlantic Coast> in Halifax relayed a distress signal received from a lifeboat. *HMCS Skeena* was the nearest vessel in the area. She immediately changed course and headed toward the lifeboat's coordinates. That lifeboat was from the *Esso Williamsburg*.

Skeena signals to *Saguenay*, "Am steering course to pass through reported position of lifeboat reference COAC's 1854Z/25, 1900 hours/25th."

Skeena then signaled COAC to ask the lifeboat to "transmit on 500 Kilocycles as I am in vicinity." At this point, *Skeena's* fuel situation began to improve and she committed to searching the area on September 25th. The men had been in the lifeboat, by this point, approximately 36 hours.

Transmissions between the lifeboat and *Skeena* are as recorded earlier in this book <See Chapter 7, Lifeboat>. The men were desperate, in need of water and medical assistance, cranking a generator to keep their radio transmitting, and calling on God and *Skeena* to get to them, before it was too late.

Unfortunately, *Skeena* was never able to sight the lifeboat. The men in the lifeboat thought they saw *Skeena* coming toward them, "We are between you and the sun," and reported sighting a vessel with one smoke stack. *Skeena*, a destroyer, had two. One of the stacks, though, was smaller than the other and it could have appeared on the horizon to a group of desperate men as a one stacked ship. The lifeboat's transmissions ended with, "The ship we see has one stack." To the end, they thought *Skeena* was close by and that rescue was at hand.

Did the transmitter fail to send more messages, so that the men were unable to communicate with *Skeena* as to their location? Or, did a rogue wave capsize the small boat and catapult them into the angry seas? This mystery will never be solved.

The courage of *HMSC Skeena's* captain <Lt. Kenneth L. Dyer, RCN> and crew deserves special recognition. At great risk to their ship and themselves, they deviated from the safe course and remained in U-boat infested waters, transmitting constantly, firing rounds of ammunition and dropping depth charges, in an effort to save a few men who were in peril on the sea. They acted in the finest tradition of seafaring men.

It should be noted that at the time of *Skeena's* search for the life-boat, Lt. Dyer was only 27-yeears-old.

Lt. Dyer went on to command the destroyer *HMCS Skootenay*. In the spring of 1942, he rescued 19 men from the Norwegian tanker *Sandanger*, who were adrift in the North Atlantic after their ship had been torpedoed and sunk by U-221. In November of 1942 he received the Distinguished Service Cross for "...gallantry during active opera-tions against the enemy at sea."

HMCS Skeena, however, did not fare well. In October of 1944, she was performing escort service off the coast of Iceland during a furious gale so typical of these dangerous North Atlantic waters. *Skeena* was ordered to take refuge in Reykjavik Harbor. The ship's anchor did not hold fast in the horrific winds that buffeted the harbor, and she was smashed up against the coast of Videy Island. The ship was lost, as well as the lives of 15 crew members, ranging in age from 19 to 30. Some of these must have been among the crew members who bravely went to the rescue of merchant mariners in these war-torn waters.

Canadian destroyer *HMCS Skeena* valiantly
tried to save the men in the lifeboat. (Canadian Navy Heritage, Public Domain)

CHAPTER TEN

GHOST SHIP

F.d.U./B.d.U.'S War Log
4. October 1942.

"U 254 sank an abandoned tanker of 8,000 GRT in AK 5561. This confirms the view that the English often just give up badly damaged ships without attempting to tow them in, as was the case in the Autumn of 1941."

In 2009, the following appeared on the web site uboat.net:

On 3 Oct, 1942, U-254 came across an abandoned and burnt out tanker, which was the drifting wreck of Esso Williamsburg. The U-boat finished her off with two coups de grâs fired at 14.32 and 14.42 hours.

This obviously contradicts all previous accounts of the demise of the *Esso Williamsburg* and thus begins a controversy involving the *Robert H. Colley*, an 11,651 ton T-2 American tanker lost out of Convoy HX-209 in October of 1942.

To begin with, major post WW II historians concluded that U-254 sank the *Robert H. Colley*.

According to Robert Browning, <U. S. War Action Casualties> on October 4, 1942 at 4:40 p.m. Otto Lowe was in command of U-254 and fired one torpedo that struck the *Robert H. Colley* "forward of the mainmast on the starboard side in the #6 tank and broke the vessel in two." The forward section of the ship sank several hours later; the after section remained afloat. At 6 a.m. the following morning,

HMS Borage came on the scene to rescue 29 men who were stranded on the *Colley's* after section.

Captain Arthur Moore <A Careless Word, A Needless Sinking> reported that the attack and sinking occurred about 350 miles south and west of Reykjavik, Iceland (59.06N/16-18W). He states that the escort vessel sank the after section by gunfire and depth charges on October 5 at 4:00 p.m. 33 survivors were carried to Londonderry, Ireland by *HMS Borage*. Two lifeboats escaped from the stern section carrying 11 men who were not heard from again.

Clay Blaire <Hitler's U-Boat War> states that Odo Lowe recorded "that he sank the burned-out hulk of the 11,700 ton abandoned American tanker *Robert H. Colley*...."

Kenneth Wynn <U-Boat Operations of the Second World War, Vol. 1> notes that the attack began on the afternoon of October 3 and the ship was reported by U-254 as "abandoned and drifting" prior to the attack.

Jurgen Rohwer <Axis Submarine Successes 1939-1945> reports the attack began at 2:32 p.m. on October 3 with the first hit occurring at 4:40 p.m. "...on the diesel tanker *Robert H. Colley* (11,651) in grid AK 5561 (59.06N/26.18W)."

The commodore of HX-209 with which the *Colley* was sailing was one W. R. B. Magee, DSO R.N.R. In his report on the loss of the *Robert H. Colley* from the convoy, Commodore Magee sends this message:

Sequel from Commodore to S. O. Escort, 7:28 a.m October 5:

Nobody onboard actually saw what occurred owing to poor visibility at that time. Both No. 61 and 72 reported that she <Robert H. Colley> had broken her back, the latter adding that no explosion was seen or heard, am asking 71. I do not consider now that she was torpedoed.

The C.O. of convoy escort vessel *HMS Highlander* reported to *Borage* after picking up survivors:

The survivors mention an explosion, a sort of a "crump". The Chief Engineer didn't consider it was a torpedo. He has been bumped once before.

The formal statement made by the *Colley's* Chief Engineer *was* cautious:

At about 4:40 p.m. on October 4th, 1942, there was an explosion on the starboard side of No. 6 tank; this was followed in a few seconds by the breaking in two of the vessel.

However, a CONFIDENTIAL Memorandum for File was written on December 15 of 1942 by Lt. Robert Fulton, USNR. The subject is <u>Summary of Statements by Survivors</u> of the *SS Robert H. Colley*.

The ROBERT H. COLLEY was torpedoed without warning at 1640, ship's time, on October 4, 1942, about 500 miles WNW of Ireland.... The ship broke in two several minutes after being struck, the aft portion being sunk by 4" shells and depth charges by H.M.S. BORAGE the next morning, the forward portion sinking of its own accord later.

The tanker was proceeding in convoy with 6 lookouts--one on the bow, 3 on the bridge, plus captain and two mates, and two gunners on the stern. At 1640, ship's time, the ship was struck by a torpedo just forward of her mainmast and almost immediately broke in two parts, the bow floating ahead and later floating aft. The submarine was not seen at any time. The comment is offered that while it was officially known one sub was in the immediate vicinity and others were approaching, the vessels in convoy were constantly showing unnecessary lights after dark.

There is no doubt that the *Robert H. Colley* broke apart and sank. The problem arises in that the "kill" was attributed to U-254 not only at the time but also in subsequent historical accounting.

Controversy over that ship's sinking evolved over decades. And the fuel for this controversy goes right back to what Doenitz noted in his report of 4.October.1942:

U 254 sank an abandoned tanker of 8,000 GRT in AK 5561.

Beginning in 2004, discussion forums on the Internet including Warsailors.com began a series of threads relating to questions about the sinking of the *Robert Colley*. Discussion starts with a query by Jan-Olof, Sweden, posted on December 7, 2004:

I am slightly confused, from looking through the sources at my disposal, regarding the loss of the U.S. tanker Robert H. Colley in early October 1942. As far as I can tell, all sources seems to agree to the following:

- She was part of convoy HX.209

- She was torpedoed by U 254

So far there are no problems here except that U 254 made her attack at 14:32 hours on 03.10.42 in AK 5561, i.e. 56N/33W. This information is found in Rohwer and other sources.

Lloyd's War Losses, Browning and others place the attack at 16:40 hours on 04.10.42 (a day later) in position 59N/26W (quite some distance from the position reported by U 254).

I can't make head or tail of this, hopefully someone else can.

Shortly thereafter responses by forum members fanned the flames of new theories.

Using <u>Lloyd's War Losses</u> as a source again, it is reported that the chief engineer onboard the *Colley* would not make a definitive statement that the ship had been torpedoed, since the explosion had been slight. Seas were rough. The *Colley* could have had her back broken by the dangerous North Atlantic waves and floated into two parts. No sub was sighted by the crew of the *Colley*.

Subsequent comments on this thread led to several theories:

- **Half of the *Colley* was sunk by convoy escort the next day, so it could not have been the abandoned tanker reported sunk by U-254;**
- **If not the *Colley*, then U-254 had to have sunk another abandoned tanker;**
- **Searches using mostly Rohwer's listings show the *Esso Williamsburg* sunk on September 23 by U-211 in the area;**
- **U-211 reported the *Williamsburg* being in two pieces and floating apart at the time it left the scene; prevailing wind and weather conditions in the North Atlantic could account for the drifting of derelict parts of the *Williamsburg* for 11 days.**

U-boat.net made the decision to accept the theory that the *Esso Williamsburg* was sunk on October 4 by U-254, and not by U-211 on September 23. This conclusion remains on their site in spite of the following facts:

- U-211 reported hitting the ship with four torpedoes, the final one hitting the starboard side and lighting the ship up in flames.
- Black smoke rose 300 feet above the ship.
- The masts tilted toward each other.
- The ship broke in two.
- The two parts floated free from each other.
- U-211 waited another hour watching the ship sinking, and reported it was still sinking as they left the scene.

That such debris could reappear again eleven days later in the apparition of an 8,000 ton tanker is dubious. Perhaps one part of the ship did not sink immediately and presented itself as an abandoned tanker to the hungry eyes of U-254?

However, the damage to the *Esso Williamsburg* reported in the log of U-211 precludes any possibility of it being an intact 8,000 ton abandoned tanker found adrift in the swirling seas of the North Atlantic. The reader can decide one way or the other.

EPILOGUE

The story of the *Esso Williamsburg* is constructed much in the same way as a tapestry is sewn, piece by piece, out of the fabrics of fact and conjecture, the whole becoming bigger than its parts. In some ways, it is a never-ending story. The author continues to find relevant bits and pieces of information that enhance the narrative.

Harry Hutson proves to be a fascinating figure. After more than a year of correspondence with Harry, I find out something that should not have surprised me, considering the quality and quantity of the letters and e-mails we exchanged. A member of the National Merchant Navy Association in the United Kingdom, Harry is the contact for its Immingham and South Humberside branch. I knew that he was actively involved in Britain's Merchant Navy Day on September 3, 2000 having received photos and his recollections of that day.

Not until "surfing" the web for new and pertinent books in the maritime genre did I find Merriam Press's website and the news that Harry is a published author and well-known source of information within that genre.

Arctic Interlude: Independent to North Russia by Harry C. Hutson recounts the voyage of 13 merchant ships, seven British, five American, and one Russian that attempted to reach North Russia from Iceland in the autumn of 1942 without escort. The publisher's web site states that:

Harry Hutson is well acquainted with the Arctic, having spent many years as a radio operator on Grimsby trawlers, fishing these same waters summer and winter.

His previous book, Grimsby's Fighting Fleet, was successfully published in the UK.

Harry's extended time and patience with a research novice like me was inspirational. He is a prominent "link" in the chain of maritime devotees it has been my good fortune to come across. Harry also contributed another piece of information that perhaps reflects what was the beginning of the end for the crew of the *Esso Williamsburg:*

Following entry in **Admiralty War Diary (Foreign Stations)**

Monday **21 Sept. 1942***, page 627. "Received at 0824 gmt from KVOF (Esso Williamsburg). Pass to Admiralty. From KVOF MSG 1 CK 73 strong distress signals were heard here all day on 600 m. at l hour and 2 hour intervals sometimes at 30 minutes after the hour and other times 45 minutes after the hour. Signals consisted of distress signal and 3 times followed by a 4 second dash and repeated for approximately 2 minutes. A blue flare was sighted at 2230 gmt 20th at 4338N 4230W. (Porteshead Radio 0834 gmt/21st to Admty, C. in C. W. A.).*

We cannot know who was the last man to die from the ship. Nevertheless, we can track his awareness of imminent death in a brief summarizing chronology:

September 21

3:40 p Tanker is sighted by U-211.

11:16.m. U-211 fires a two-torpedo spread and hits EW. Ship escapes in fog.

September 22

19:19 a.m. Tanker again sighted by U-211.

10: p.m. Single torpedo fired, hits amidships.

10:36 pm. Another torpedo fired, misses ship.

EPILOGUE

11:05 p.m. Another torpedo fired, ship breaks in two.

Midnight U-211 leaves scene with tanker still sinking.

September 23   Men in lifeboat.

September 24 Men in lifeboat.

September 25

554 p.m. First transmission received from EW lifeboat.

September 26

6:10 p.m. Last transmission received from EW lifeboat.

The last crewmember of the *Esso Williamsburg* looked death in the eye for almost six full days. He lived through the gruesome knowledge that submarines were operating in the area in which they were sailing, and that other mariners were "out there" in ships or lifeboats, calling desperately for help. Whether they were aware of being shadowed by U-211 we shall never know. This last crewmember lived through the first attack, during which his ship was hit twice by torpedoes. For the next 12 hours, he sailed on a ship filled with highly volatile Navy fuel that limped alone through the fog, sustaining damage from two direct hits. Then, just when he thought they were outrunning the sub, lightning strikes again when a single torpedo hits the center of his ship. 39 minutes later another torpedo breaks his ship in two.

Even so, he was "lucky" to get into a lifeboat. For more than two days he is in that lifeboat with men who are desperately sending out distress signals. The boat is swamped. He needs water and medical assistance. Finally, a destroyer answers the lifeboat's desperate pleas and is coming to the rescue.

Twenty-four hours later, the sun comes out. He sees the destroyer in the distance. Their calls are being answered. The ship is close; they can make out its configuration.

Did he survive the presumed last swamping of the lifeboat? Did he float around in the water, only to drown while watching the destroyer and salvation slowly approaching? We don't know how long it took the destroyer to reach the wreckage of the lifeboat. How many hours of suffering were added to this man's existence?

Yet, in the scheme of things, this was "business as usual" in the North Atlantic during World War II, particularly during the years 1942 and 1943. From all accounts published, we know that rafts, lifeboats, and live and dead men in lifejackets floated freely on these waters, the flotsam and jetsam of a heinous battle.

The last man to die from the crew of the *Esso Williamsburg* was just one more soul of thousands.

As for the men of the U-211, one can ask, "Did their families not suffer as greatly as ours?" Did not the family of 19-year-old Werner Fellmuth suffer as much as the family of 19-year-old Fred McLee Jones on learning of their deaths? Did Kapitanleutnant zur See (KL) Karl Hause have a young daughter who had nightmares about *his* death?

Perhaps they too were caught up in this unrequited love of country, theirs a misplaced patriotism. They were sent out to almost certain death by their government. That they were a courageous lot operating in sub-human conditions cannot be denied, and all for the monomania of the Kriegsmarine: tonnage sunk. And most of them paid the ultimate price themselves. Only a few were transferred off U-211 before it met its end.

As for my father, I believe he symbolizes the men who sailed the merchant ships in World War II. Risk was the way of his life. Moreover, as a naturalized American citizen, he greatly loved his adopted country.

The United States Government, however, treated the men of the U. S. Merchant Marine and their Navy Armed Guard shipmates as pawns and cannon fodder. In spite of this, innocence existed in my father's sense of duty.

"We have the licenses, and we must go," he told my mother. He also thought that his adopted country had been good to him. I am certain that he died still believing.

Will the world see men like those of the *Esso Williamsburg* and U-211 again? I think not. In United States history, the World War II era stands out as the last bastion of egalitarian patriotism. Described as the "greatest generation," the men and women of this time survived the Great Depression only to be catapulted into a world war of monumental proportions. Husbands, fathers, and sons from all walks of life went willingly into the service of their country. Wives, mothers, and daughters fought on the home front, working in factories, knitting sweaters and socks for the troops, writing letters, and stand-ing as symbols of why the war was being fought.

Had these men and women been given the opportunity to see world conditions as they really were, had they lived in an age of instant news, would things have been different? Today we see war in real time, as it is being waged. It makes us no wiser as individuals as to the price of war. America's greatest generation will never return. The farmer fought with the patrician, side by side, forming unbreak-able bonds.

Now, cable news and the advent of the Internet are forging new generations of informed citizens who see first-hand the wages of war and who are the most politically educated in the history of the world. Yet, few are now involved in our military conflict.

War for most 21st century Americans citizens is a spectator sport. Citizens trapped within war-torn countries now have methods of instant communication with the outside world. We now know more *about* war than any of our predecessors. Yet war continues.

Was my father on board the lifeboat? I believe so. I believe this by virtue of the same intuition that worked within me when I was four-years-old and dreamt of his standing on the deck of a burning ship shortly before the *Esso Williamsburg* went missing. I am as sure now that my father was in the lifeboat, as I was at the age of four that his ship was burning. And I'm left to wonder if this is beyond doubt the end of the story of the *Esso Williamsburg*.

Truly in my heart I expect that one day the doorbell will ring, the front door will open briskly, and he will be standing there, a rela-tively young man with auburn hair, blue eyes, and the deep tan of those who go to sea—his uniform covered with verdigris, drenched as though just arisen from the sea, once more returned, after a seventy year voyage.

Northport, New York
September 1, 2011

Memorial plaque for Hans Andreasen,
Calverton National Cemetery,
Long Island, New York. (Andreasen Family)

Memorial for Henry F. Lehde, Texas.
(Arthur Mohr)

Memorial for Lea M. Gayle, Texas.
(Arthur Mohr)

ADDENDUM

This story would not be complete without additional information on the master of the *Esso Williamsburg*, Lieutenant Commander John Tweed, U. S. Navy Reserve. Unfortunately, over many years of research, the author was unable to contact any surviving members of Captain Tweed's family. What follows is gleaned from the National Archives, U. S. Armed Guard files, and several pertinent publications, such as <u>Ships of the Esso Fleet in World War II</u>.

John Tweed was born in DeKalb, Illinois on December 8, 1896. His father was born in Stavanger, Norway. At the time of his death in 1942, he was 46-years-old. DeKalb is not far from Chicago and the Great Lakes, so the assumption is made that he began his sailing career on those waters. From there he made his way to the East Coast. The first official record we have of his career shows residence in Greenwich, New Jersey in 1915, when he was licensed as an "operator of motor vessels." He was then 19-years-old.

Four years later, then residing in Boston, Massachusetts, he became an officer for the first time. He made 3rd Mate at the age of 23 and sailed on the Standard Oil Company's tanker *L. J. Drake*. A little over a year later, he became 2nd Mate on the tanker *J. A. Moffitt*. Two years later, he was Chief Mate of this vessel. Finally, in 1923, he became Master of the *H. M. Flagler*. He was 27-years-old and in command of a 12,480 ton oil tanker.

In the late 1920's, he moved to Staten Island, New York, where so many merchant mariners resided with their families. Home was then just a short shuttle ride away from the Standard Oil refineries in Bayway and Bayonne, New Jersey via the Kill van Kull motor launch.

For the next ten years, he was the master of several tankers, including the *E. M Clark* and the *Thomas H. Wheeler*. His last command, of course, was the *Esso Williamsburg*. By this time, his residence was listed as Jackson Heights, Queens, New York with his wife and next-of-kin, Florence Tweed.

In June of 1942, when he joined the *Esso Williamsburg*, Captain Tweed had only three months left in his life. What we know of that time is reflected in the movements of the *Esso Williamsburg*. The ship made two major crossings of the Atlantic Ocean through enemy waters to Glasgow, Scotland and Liverpool, England. During this period, they followed all the wartime regulations set forth for merchant vessels. Tweed's job was to navigate quickly and safely through submarine-infested waters with his ship's precious cargo: oil.

Captain Tweed's record is exemplary. We know from Captain Arthur Moore's report on the recollections of "old-timers," i.e., ex Esso ((Standard Oil) skippers, that Captain Tweed "...got one or two boats in the water probably before the final torpedo." Heard by several ships was his final message, "We are heading into the Sun." It is likely that Captain Tweed remained with the ship and went down with her in the proud tradition of sea captains.

RESOURCES

"Am I Still Steering for You?" The Crowsnest, <The Royal Canadian Navy's Magazine> Vol. 9 No. 4, February 1957, pp. 17-18.

Blair, Clay. Hitler's U-Boat War. New York: Random House, 1998.

Browning, Robert Jr. U. S. Merchant Vessel War Casualties of World War II. Annapolis: Naval Institute Press, 1996.

Bunker, John G. Heroes in Dungarees: The Story of the American Merchant Marine in World War II. Annapolis: Naval Institute Press, 1995.

Carse, Robert. The Long Haul, The U.S. Merchant Service in World War II. New York: W. W. Norton & Company, Inc., 1965.

Edwards, Bernard. Donitz and the Wolf Packs, The U-Boats at War. London: Cassell Military Classics, 1996.

Gannon, Michael. Black May. New York: HarperCollins Publishers, Inc., 1989.

Hutson, Harry C. Arctic Interlude, Independent to North Russia. Bennington: Merriam Press, 1997.

Lloyd's War Losses, The Second World War 1939-45: 3 September 1939-14 August   (V 1), Lloyds's of London.

Moore, Arthur R. A Careless Word, A Needless Sinking. Dennis A. Roland Chapter of New Jersey of the American Merchant Marine Veterans, 1998.

Reed, James H. Convoy "Maniac": R.B.1. England: Book Guild Ltd., 2000.

Rohwer, Jurgen. Axis Submarine Successes 1939-1945. Annapolis: United States Naval Institute Press, 1983.

Ships of the Esso Fleet in World War II. Standard Oil Company (New Jersey), 1946.

Summary of Merchant Marine Personnel Casualties, World War II. Washington: United States Government Printing Office, 1950. <CG 228, July 1, 1950>.

Wynn, Kenneth. **U-Boat Operations of the Second World War, Volume 1: Career Histories, U-1-510.** Annapolis: Naval Institute Press, 1997.

Internet

http://usmm.org/shipmate_search.html
http://www.merriam-press.com/m_219_author.html,
Ray Merriam
http://www.uboatarchive.net/BDUKTB.htm

F.d.U./B.d.U.'S War Log, Des Führers/Befehlshaber der Unterseeboote (F.d.U./B.d.U.) War Diary and War Standing Orders of Commander in Chief, Submarines. <The original translated BdU KTBs are in the custody of the Operational Archives Branch of the Naval Historical Center located at the Navy Yard in Washington, D.C.>

http://uboatarchive.net/ESFWarDiaryFeb42APP4.htm

U. S. Navy Eastern Sea Frontier Diary

http://www.hmsfiredrake.co.uk/firedrake5.htm4

Donald J. L. Coombes eye witness report on the sinking of the destroyer HMS Firedrake.

http://www.hmsfiredrake.co.uk/firedrake13.htm

John Dixon and Peter Collins eye witness reports on the sinking of the Destroyer HMS Firedrake.

http://www.hmsfiredrake.co.uk/firedrake23.htm

Lt. D. J. Dampier, RN eye witness report on the sinking of the destroyer HMS Firedrake.

http://warsailors.com/forum/search.php?1,search=Robert+H.+C olley,page=1,matchtype=ALL,matchdates=0,match_forum=ALL
http://uboat.net/allies/merchants/ships/2203.html
Ships Hit by U-boats, *Esso Williamsburg.*

Archives
Library and Archives Canada. Ship's log- *Skeena*, **R112-491-3-E, volumes 7858-7861.**

German U-Boat Museum (Deutsches U-Boot Museum) <previously U-Boat Archives> Altenbrucher Bahnhofstrasse 57, 27478 Cuxhaven, Germany, Horst Bredow, Founder.

U. S. National Archives, Washington, D.C.

U. S. Naval Armed Guard file, *Esso Williamsburg.*

Armed Guard Report - *Robert H. Colley* **on or about October 3, 1942, box 558.**

U. S. National Archives and Records Administration, Civil Reference.

Staff Archives II, Records Group 242, College Park, MD_ <U-211 log>

ABOUT THE AUTHOR

Norma Andreasen taught English and writing in private and public schools for thirty years. Now a retired English chairperson, she has been researching and writing about World War II and the Battle of the North Atlantic for decades. The unraveling of a family mystery became her key to understanding the importance of that battle in the winning World War II. She now lives on the North Shore of Long Island, New York.

11173914R00074

Made in the USA
Charleston, SC
04 February 2012